DISCOURSE, POWER AND RESISTANCE

CHALLENGING THE RHETORIC OF CONTEMPORARY EDUCATION

WITHDRAWN

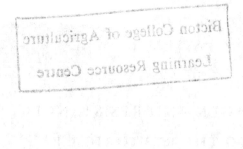

Discourse, Power and Resistance

CHALLENGING THE RHETORIC
OF CONTEMPORARY EDUCATION

edited by Jerome Satterthwaite
Elizabeth Atkinson
and Ken Gale

Trentham Books
Stoke on Trent, UK and Sterling USA

Trentham Books Limited

Westview House	22883 Quicksilver Drive
734 London Road	Sterling
Oakhill	VA 20166-2012
Stoke on Trent	USA
Staffordshire	
England ST4 5NP	

First published 2003

British Library Cataloguing-in-Publication Data
A catalogue record for this book is available from the British Library

ISBN 1 85856 299 6

Designed and typeset by Trentham Print Design Ltd., Chester and printed in Great Britain by Cromwell Press Ltd., Wiltshire.

Contents

Foreword

GORDON TAYLOR

Head of the School of Graduate Studies, University of Plymouth

In summer 2000 colleagues in the School of Graduate Studies at the University of Plymouth formed themselves into a small research team to look at trends in post-compulsory education and training, taking as the focus of their work the words *discourse, power* and *resistance*. They quickly developed links with colleagues in other Higher Education institutions world-wide; and in April 2002 brought delegates to the first conference on what had already become known as 'DPR', entitled 'Discourse, Power and Resistance in Post-Compulsory Education and Training'. The conference launched a major debate, and is set to become an annual event, providing a forum for the discussion of new directions in all sectors of education.

Drawing on papers presented at the conference, this book takes forward the discussion of issues that are urgent for all of us – academics, students and managers – who are engaged in the processes of education. It is published at a moment when theories and practices of teaching are being called to increasingly strict account. The scope is international, interdisciplinary and cross-phase, bringing together a range of voices from the international education community who share a common concern to engage with issues of discourse, power and resistance in the context of educational policy, practice and research.

Introduction

JEROME SATTERTHWAITE

This book is a reworking of papers given at the conference 'Discourse, Power and Resistance in Post-Compulsory Education and Training' held in Plymouth, UK, in April 2002.

The book is divided into two parts. In the first, the authors examine the way we as academics and teachers are discursively constructed by contemporary political and educational rhetoric, and how we offer resistance through the analysis of a range of discourses of power. As Helen Colley puts it in the closing chapter of Part One:

> Liberating possibilities are offered simply through the act of naming a regime of truth. Naming a discourse can challenge unconscious acceptance of it, and enable resistance to its disciplinary function.

This challenge informs the analyses offered in Part One which resist the view that power operates above and beyond us, through the discourses of quality assurance, to construct us as a workforce training a workforce, doing and telling what we are told, and training students to do the same. These chapters recognise and expose the rocks and hard places between which contemporary education is increasingly crushed. But victimhood is not commended in these analyses; what these chapters urge – in perspectives ranging from traditional to postmodern – is that we look carefully at contemporary trends in education, taking the trouble to understand the discourse and the power it brings to bear, so that resistance is effective.

Part Two then reverses the polarity. Are not the teachers, the academics, themselves also oppressors? Higher education has traditions reaching back to a past where élitism – and the exclusivity that goes with it – was celebrated. Education, clerical, classical and preoccupied with ideas and ideals, elevated its graduates – the doctors and masters of Philosophy, Divinity and Law (and, perhaps more grudgingly, of Medicine) – to the status of custodians of a knowledge on which civilisation was thought to depend for its preservation. This was high knowledge: graduates had climbed steps, taken degrees and higher degrees, each stage in their progression marked by uplifting ceremonial. They had entered the academy, separating themselves from the vulgar, whose common knowledge was the practical barbarism they were now privileged to despise.

The chapters in Part Two direct attention to the assumptions and practices of contemporary academic education, finding widespread evidence that these élitist assumptions die hard. Exclusivity persists, and produces frustrations and humiliations in education at all levels but perhaps particularly for those seeking what is still termed 'higher education'. These chapters expose and face the facts about contemporary educational discourses, the power associated with them, and the strategies of resistance they produce, as we struggle to get things right.

There are no easy solutions in this book; there are hard questions and clear recognitions, intended to promote the kind of indiscipline, which, paradoxically, is a trained response, thoughtfully articulated.

PART ONE

PART ONE

1

Education, postmodernism and the organisation of consent

ELIZABETH ATKINSON

Elizabeth Atkinson parades an army of postmodern thinkers before the reader, and suggests that they have much to offer in terms of resistance to the rhetoric of standards, improvement and best practice. In a characteristically postmodern move, Atkinson laughs in the face of the policy-makers with deeply serious intent. Her theme is taken up again throughout this book, particularly in Hursh's analysis of governmentality in New York, and in the unsettling of political and intellectual certainties offered by Quinn, Colley, Gale and White.

Introduction

In this chapter, I present postmodern critique as a powerful tool for unsettling the excessive certainties of contemporary educational discourse. I argue that postmodern thinking provides rich material for a form of resistance which goes beyond uneasy compliance and fretful complaint, and challenges the structures through which we collude with the rhetoric of standards, improvement and best practice. My aim is to challenge régimes of truth; to make strange the certainties on which power/knowledge in education rests; and to dis-organise – through giving voice to counter-discourses and to silenced texts – the organisation of consent on which current educational policy and practice rest. Set in the context of initial training for primary teachers in the UK, the resistance to contemporary discourses proposed here reaches beyond primary teacher training into every area of education and crosses geographical borders.

Education and postmodernism: pitting the certain against the uncertain?

This chapter aims is to persuade you, the reader, that postmodern thinking has much to offer as a form of resistance in the contemporary educational climate. It explores the notion that we are trapped, in education, within régimes of truth against which postmodern thinking has much to offer as a form of resistance. Why postmodernism? Perhaps I was born too late – too late for full-blown Marxism, or for the excitement and stir of second-wave feminism; too late, too, for postmodernism if I'd been in the field of arts or literature, architecture, cultural studies or sociology. But education moves slowly – very slowly, in terms of thinking about itself, and excessively fast, of course, in terms of policies and initiatives – and this creates a vacuum in which the arrogant discourse of 'what works' and 'best practice' seems to find itself comfortably unopposed by counter-discourse. This, I think, is where postmodernism has a role to play – in stirring up these excessive certainties, and offering some thinking from the margins to counteract the gravitational pull of the centre.

So I want to parade before you my troupe of seriously playful combatants, armed with irony, subversion and the refusal to take anything for granted. On my right – geographically speaking and provided I stand mid-Atlantic and face North – Ian Stronach and Maggie MacLure from the UK. On my left, from the US, Patti Lather – Amazon of Academia – and her fellow warriors, Deborah Britzman and Elizabeth St. Pierre, accompanied by Gayatri Spivak, Judith Butler and a host of others. And behind them all, and speaking through them, as though, in Peggy Kamuf's words (1991) 'between the blinds', Messieurs Jacques Derrida and Michel Foucault, those self-denied Grand Narrators of a way of thinking that denies Grand Narratives, bringing with them all the acceptance of ironies that that position implies. I want to show you how these writers, my knights of multiplicity, have my favour in the joust – or is it the jest – against 'what works', 'best practice', and that curiously doom-laden phrase, 'excellence in education'.

Picture the scene. A five-year-old reveals that she cannot segment a word into phonemes; a class of ten-year-olds fails to identify complex

4

sentences; a trainee teacher does not know how many minutes constitute the second section of the literacy hour.[1] Shocked eyebrows are raised. Questions are asked. Care is needed here: Ofsted[2] are on their way, and heads may roll. An institution's future is at stake: either the trainee, or her trainers, may be judged to be non-compliant . . . At another institution, another trainee (not a student: we don't have those in the professions) wrestles with clusters and digraphs; a third marks off Standards 3biii and 5dvi in *High Status, High Standards: Requirements for Courses of Initial Teacher Training* (Department for Education and Employment 1998a[3]). Every 'i' must be dotted; every 't' crossed. Failure to meet every Standard will mean failure to enter the profession. It is not a question of *relative* or *partial* merit or competence: it is either yes or no. This is the régime of truth in which I exist in Initial Teacher Training. And I don't like it.

What can postmodern thinking offer against this nightmare surrealism? This day-in-day-out, government-driven, initiatives-led, inspection-accounted-for simulacrum of education in which we exist? How can postmodernism enable us to resist what Marilyn Strathern (2000) calls 'the tyranny of transparency'? How can it help us to counter that invidious accountability which defines everything we should know and do in order to prove that we don't know it, and can't do it? How can we pit the ludic – the playful, the ironic, the restless, shape-shifting dance of postmodernism – against the ludicrous?

Well, laughing wouldn't be a bad start. How often have you laughed in recent staff meetings, as you've incorporated the latest government initiative into your own particular field of education? And how often do you laugh as you try to reconcile those initiatives with the counter-discourses of your own thinking? Maybe laughing would be a *good* start. Maybe a bit of Carnival is what we need. Why not shout *O le le* to the policy-makers? Turn all the norms upside down? Take to the streets and proclaim that the Emperor has no clothes? Why not stand up and be counted? But *O le le* is not enough: like the dispossessed of Brazil who parade the streets once a year at Carnival, and like their enslaved West African ancestors who kept their rhythms going even when the drums were banned, we are still trapped, still dancing at the end of the puppeteer's strings, still enslaved in the rhetoric of Standards, Excellence and Improvement.

Well, you might ask, what's wrong with Standards? What's wrong with Excellence? What's wrong with Improvement? If I don't like the heat, why don't I just get out of the kitchen? What, for goodness' sake, is my problem? My problem is this: I don't believe in this stuff; and I don't believe in the *requirement* to believe in it. And worse, I don't believe in what I am doing to maintain, perpetuate and reproduce it. Deborah Britzman and Don Dippo (2000: 33) state:

> Teacher education must always waiver between the poles of hope for the future – that one's efforts in education can matter to the quality of lives lived – and, despair toward one's own present, who one is becoming as one initiates and responds to the expectations, demands, and pressures of curriculum, neighbourhood, and nation.

This wavering between poles is not a healthy activity; and I don't like who I'm becoming in the process, particularly in response to the rhetoric of policy, inspection and professional standards. It's tearing me in two (see Atkinson 2000a). So I want to try messing things up instead.

Why use postmodernism to do this? Because some sort of radical unsettling is needed in education when thinking outside the box has become a sort of heresy. Try talking about literacy outside the terms of the literacy hour. Try talking about post-16 achievement outside the terms of Key Skills, GNVQs, or Curriculum 2000.[4] Try talking about education itself outside the terms of Standards, Excellence and Improvement. Other ways of thinking and knowing, other languages for describing, other tongues for speaking have become so silent, so invisible, that we have almost forgotten their existence. Postmodernism may not be in the business of providing answers, but it's certainly in the business of asking questions, and that's one of the things I like about it. As Britzman and Dippo put it (2000: 31):

> The future of a profession resides in the questions it might ask of itself and how such questions affect its thinking . . .[T]he question . . . can inhibit curiosity, increase defensiveness, and protect the questioner from implication. It can also take our knowledge by surprise, provoke interesting thinking, new conversations, and transformations of knowledge.

This is the sort of question I am interested in. In an era overtaken by 'the dominance of visuality,' as Ian Stronach puts it (1999) where 'the

6

seeing drums out the interpreting, and we experience the accidental death of educational philosophy', this is the sort of question that we need.

Postmodernism and the knights of multiplicity

Postmodernism is not the only way of thinking that unsettles certainties – in education or elsewhere. I have repeatedly acknowledged the part played by feminist, Marxist, postcolonial and queer theory in unsettling certainties and disrupting easy complacency (see, for example, Atkinson 2000b, 2002a, 2002b). But in a world where, in the words of Stephen Ball (2001a) 'we are invited to shed our contingent histories and sign up to orthodoxy,' I like the way that postmodernism recognises those contingent histories; how it allows for the diversity and difference which accompanies our attempts at ways of knowing; how it listens to the voices from the margins and resists the seduction of the centre. I like the way in which postmodern thinkers resist certainty and resolution; accept lack of clarity and the complications of multiplicity; acknowledge subjectivity, contradiction and irony; and refuse to accept boundaries and binary opposites. And I like it because it's fun.

So how can postmodernism help us to break out into a new, different and less predictable dance, with less of the conformist and more of the carnivalesque about it? This is where my knights of multiplicity come in. Not all of them, to be sure, would describe themselves as postmodernists – some would prefer to be described as poststructuralists or feminist poststructuralists, while others, notably Derrida and Foucault, resist labelling of any kind. But 'postmodernism' will do nicely to encapsulate the ways of thinking which bring my heroes together, rather than those which might divide them. I have even dared to recruit my favourite not-at-all postmodernist (at least by his own definition) to my cause: Jerome Bruner, whose refusal to box and constrain ways of thinking has led me to open a paper entitled 'What can postmodern thinking do for educational research?' (Atkinson 2000c) with his wonderful words from *On Knowing* (1979: 18):

> My antic sense rises in self-defence. My advice, in the midst of the seriousness, is to keep an eye out for the tinker shuffle, the flying of kites, and kindred sources of surprised amusement.

But back to postmodernism proper – a contradiction in terms if ever there was one. What can my trusty band of warriors, by now thoroughly frustrated at waiting in the sidelines for so long, and increasingly irritated at being described in such modernist terms, offer to help us out of the impasse education finds itself in?

Well, Derrida writes of resistance towards violent hierarchies and binary oppositions (1976: 41) a resistance towards the polarity of either/or thinking. Stronach and MacLure (1997: 5) bring a reading of Derrida (among others) to a range of contemporary situations, identifying ways in which postmodern thinkers 'choose *not* to choose between [such oppositions], *not* to work to transcend them nor, importantly, to ignore them, but instead to complicate the relations *between* them'. Postmodernism invites us to complicate the relations between the good/bad, success/failure, compliant/non-compliant rhetoric of education policy as a way of moving away from simplistic and unproductive binaries in an undeniably complex world.

Derrida writes too (1976) of 'writing *sous-rature*' – crossing words out even as they are used – to acknowledge the constraints and inadequacy of language (within which the discourses of education are included) while at the same time recognising that we are inevitably trapped within it. And he writes of deconstruction not as a method or an approach but as something that 'takes place everywhere' (1987: 274), that 'borrows from a heritage the resources necessary for the de-construction of that heritage itself' (1978: 289). This, surely, is something we find ourselves bound to do in any critique of educational policy or practice, or of any other social institution: something Peggy Kamuf describes (1991: viii) as 'assuming responsibility for what cannot be avoided.' 'Deconstruction,' says Kamuf, 'is one name Derrida has given to this responsibility.'

Responsibility, anarchy and the organisation of consent

This idea of responsibility is one that comes up surprisingly often in a way of thinking which has been variously described as 'relativistic, nihilistic, apolitical, amoral, deliberately obfuscatory,' as another o f my knights, Elizabeth St. Pierre, puts it (2001a: 1) and it's an idea that I explore myself at length elsewhere (Atkinson 2002a). Here is Stronach and MacLure's idea of the postmodern thinker as 'the

8

responsible anarchist ... standing against the fantasies of grand narratives, recoverable pasts, and predictable futures' (1997: 98): an anarchist who names and questions the régimes of truth which frame identity and experience.

Foucault's description of régimes of truth sounds uncomfortably like the perpetuation of contemporary discourses in education:

> 'Truth' is to be understood as a system of ordered procedures for the production, regulation, distribution, circulation and operation of statements. 'Truth' is linked in a circular relation with systems of power which produce and sustain it, and to effects of power which it induces and which extend it. A régime of truth.
>
> (in Rabinow (ed) 1984: 74)

Thomas Popkewitz (2000) takes up this idea of 'effects of power' within contemporary educational discourses, while McCarthy and Dimitriades (2000) take up another Foucauldian idea, that of governmentality, whereby power is distributed through 'a decentred system of networks' involving constant self-surveillance. Doesn't this sound like education? And here is the organisation of consent: the collusion in our own oppression, which matches so well with Gramsci's concept of hegemony (1971) – a concept which has been taken up repeatedly and richly by postmodern writers. And who, in education, are the brokers and reproducers of the violent hierarchies between policy and practice, between success and failure, between compliance and non-compliance? I am. You are. We are. *We* guarantee that the new measures are put into place. *We* provide the evidence that perpetuates our accountability. *We* ensure that Standards are met – and raised. Through the pervasive and persuasive force of hegemony, we have become the agents of our own silence.

Foucault writes, too, of unmasking the apparent neutrality of those institutions which generate and circulate régimes of truth:

> The real political task in a society such as ours is to criticise the workings of institutions which appear to be both neutral and independent; to criticise them in such a manner that the political violence which has always exercised itself obscurely through them will be unmasked, so that one can fight them.
>
> (in Rabinow (ed) 1984: 6)

Again, hardly a nihilistic stance – and again that whiff of political and social responsibility. As Donna Landry and Gerald MacLean put it in their comments on their edited collection of the works of Gayatri Spivak: 'If deconstruction cannot found a political program; if Foucault's analysis of power is not a blueprint for resistance, alternative lifestyles, or social justice, of what use is a Derrida or a Foucault for doing ethico-political criticism?' (1996: 141). And, as I have confessed elsewhere (see Atkinson 2000a, 2002b) ethico-political criticism – or critical postmodernism, is what I am aiming to do.

Patti Lather (1991: 39) writes about 'producing knowledge from which to act.' Here, again, is that sense of responsibility. Elizabeth St. Pierre writes (1997a: 175) of 'producing different knowledge and producing knowledge differently'; of 'jamming the dialectical machine' (2001b: 3); and of 'the irruption of transgressive data' (1997a) – 'irruption' referring to bursting or breaking in, and transgressive data being those ways of seeing, recognising and recording experience which lie outside the norms of conventional wisdom or common sense. All these thoughts seem, to me, to provide rich resources for resistance. And once again, the theme of responsibility arises in St. Pierre's writing (2001b: 2–3):

> As Caputo [1993: 4] reminds us, 'deconstruction offers no excuse not to act.' Deconstruction interrogates the various structures we create linguistically and materially. We create binaries, hierarchies, and other grids with our language that have very real, material effects on people's lives. Such binary oppositions are possible only within a certain mode of intelligibility, a certain régime of truth.

And so to Deborah Britzman:

> Poststructuralist theories disrupt any desire for a seamless narrative, a cohesive identity, or a mimetic representation. . . These positions undermine the ethnographic belief that 'reality' is somehow out there waiting to be captured by language.
>
> (1995: 232)

I am afraid of seamless narratives: they speak too much of the frayed edges which they inevitably conceal; of what must have been forgotten, in Maggie MacLure's words (1996: 283) 'in order to tell these smooth stories of the self.'

So postmodern thinkers invite us to replace naïve certainty with a radical uncertainty, or with what St. Pierre (1997b) calls 'a most rigorous confusion'. We are invited not to ask 'the question that shuts down the trouble,' as Britzman and Dippo put it (2000: 32) but to engage with what they call 'awful thoughts;' the difficult thinking that education – like any human situation – presents. Maggie MacLure (1999) recommends that we replace easy readings and simple thoughts with a 'critical illiteracy' in research and writing which refuses to simplify or dumb down.

In our acceptance of educational certainties, simple truths about 'what works' and – perhaps worst of all – 'common sense,' we have become like the people of Aramanth in William Nicholson's chilling novel, *The Wind Singer* (2000): 'striving harder, reaching higher, to make tomorrow better than today'. And what are we going to do about it?

> Kestrel [*our girl-hero*] came to a stop at last, at the foot of the wind singer [*an ancient tower of metal tubes whose purpose had long been forgotten*]. Her rage at Pinpin's test [*her younger sister's base-line assessment*] and Dr. Batch's taunts [*her teacher's punishment for non-compliance with the rules of the classroom*], and the whole suffocating order of Aramanth, had formed within her into a wild desire to upset, to confuse, to shock – she hardly knew who or what or how – just to fracture the smooth and seamless running of the world, if only for a moment. She had come to the wind singer because it was her friend and ally, but it was only when she stood at its foot that she knew what she was going to do. She started to climb. . .
>
> 'I HA-A-ATE SCHOO-OO-OOL!' cried Kestrel's amplified voice. 'I HA-A-ATE RA-A-ATINGS!' . . . WON'T STRIVE HAR-AR-ARDER! WON'T REACH HI-I-IGHER! WON'T MAKE TOMORROW-OW-OW BETTER THAN TODAY-AY-AY!'
>
> (Nicholson, 2000: 32–37)

The questions that shut down the trouble

So what are the questions that shut down the trouble? What are the questions that flow naturally from the mouth of the policy machine? How about these as an example?

- How do you ensure that all learning outcomes are both assessable and assessed?

- How do you ensure that you are teaching exactly the right subject knowledge?
- How do you ensure that your trainees have met all the required Standards as identified by the appropriate regulating body?

And the questions – the counter-discourses – that open it up? How about these?

- What and where are the textual silences in all this policy rhetoric?
- What meanings are implied by their own absence in slogans like 'achieving excellence,' 'raising standards' and 'improving schools'?
- What can policymakers possibly mean by combinations of words like 'professionalism and trust' (Morris 2001) when the terms by which one is defined denies the possibility of the other?
- And what has happened, in the midst of all this, to the ownership of knowledge? Whose knowledge counts?

What do I want? I want more than Carnival – more than *O le le* once a year. I want to hear the voices from the margins; to ask the questions which arise from uncertainty, hybridity and multiplicity. I want to speak the unspeakable and have awful thoughts. I want to ask the questions that open up the trouble. I want, in the words of Britzman and Dippo (2000: 34) 'to risk thinking again and again.'

Notes

1. Since the introduction of the National Literacy Strategy in 1998, almost every primary school in England has followed the daily literacy hour, consisting of highly structured teaching at word, sentence and text level, following a prescribed framework of objectives (Department for Education and Employment 1998b).
2. Ofsted: the Office for Standards in Education: the regulatory body which inspets schools and initial teacher training in England and Wales.
3. Ironically, the government (through the new Department for Education and Skills) has now brought in new Standards for initial teacher training (DfES/TTA 2002) with much less focus on detail, and much more focus on diversity and inclusion: another discourse which merits critical investigation.
4. Even as I write, the particular frameworks by which teaching and learning are policed are changing: the notion of a set of Key Skills which underpin all learning; or of Competencies defined in terms of General National Vocational Qualifications; or of a National Curriculum which, among other things, redefines the qualifications for university entry; already seem old-fashioned in comparison with FENTO (Further Education/National Training Organisation) Standards for FE teaching or the new developments in student profiling at all levels. So the picture continues to change; and we continue to run to keep up with it.

2

Learning to comply;
learning to contest

STEPHEN ROWLAND

Stephen Rowland argues for critical dialogue between education and society and between learner and teacher. He sees this as a robust exchange, demanding from both sides a willingness to listen and to learn, so that the ownership of knowledge is democratic, transgressing disciplinary boundaries – inclusive in the best senses of the word. Rowland's argument here is close to Hayes' in insisting that learning is demanding: a process of strenuous engagement where meanings are won through the bringing together of minds and projects – an argument which is returned to in Satterthwaite's chapter, with its discussion of Levinas' Other.

Introduction

Academics are cajoled, criticised and pressurised to change, innovate and adapt, rather than celebrate their achievements or cherish academic values. Compliance, rather than rational debate, predominates in our institutions. Even the way we organise our basic 'product' – knowledge – is changing as the disciplines are being reshaped, and the very concept of the discipline is challenged. While there are some exciting opportunities and developments, there is also a deeply disturbing trend which risks undermining the whole enterprise.

There was never a Golden Age when the pursuit of educational ideals was an easy ride, and it could not be so. As Confucius put it: 'No vexation, no enlightenment; no anxiety, no illumination' (quoted in

Huang 1997). Learning is, to some extent, a vexatious and anxious business. It is inevitably a struggle to create, maintain and enhance the climate for learning. That struggle is a fundamental part of learning itself, not merely an unfortunate condition to be resolved *before* learning can take place.

The relationship between compliance and contestation has much to do with how we understand learning: what kind of thing it is, how it happens and what its purposes might be. In discussing these matters my focus will be on the learning of students, lecturers, research workers and others who support the enterprise: indeed the whole learning community (Schuller 1995: 44–50).

Education as a critical service

In the days when the church was the most powerful social institution, universities served its needs by preserving the doctrine and training clerics. Later, throughout the period of imperial expansion, universities took on a major function of training the élite – the administrators and the leading professionals – and providing much of the scientific knowledge that underpinned the industrial revolution. Now we are moving into a period where, according to commentators such as Klein (2001) and Hertz (2001), the major source of power in our post industrial society is no longer the church or even the state but the global economy. The global knowledge based economy now shapes higher education. The *New Rulers of the World* (Pilger 2002) are the globally oriented transnational corporations or, if one accepts Pilger's analysis, the single superpower whose military capability supports their interests. Universities now serve these economic interests. National governments are becoming little more than the means by which these global interests are served.

While the distribution of power in society has changed, the relationship of service between the university and society has not. As before, social, economic and political forces ensure that universities (like other institutions) serve the needs of society. As before, we live in a society in which power and influence are far from equal. Universities are therefore inevitably constrained to serve the powerful forces within society – be they the church, the nation state or the global economy. In that respect, they are under pressure to comply.

This simple analysis, however, is in tension with an opposing way of looking at the role of the university. The roots of this opposing view can be traced back through John Dewey (1939) to the Enlightenment of the 18th Century, or even further back to the Greek traditions of scholarship explored by Plato and Aristotle.

According to this opposing view, the role of the academy has always been to critique existing knowledge and contest the assumptions and the social forces that shape ways of thinking. It is through reason, careful observation and critical analysis that universities contribute to freeing society from the forces of unreason and prejudice. The role of the university, from this point of view, is not to serve the needs of the powerful, but to liberate us through the power of critical reasoning. The university, through scholarship, enables us not so much to serve and comply with the world as we find it, but to contest what we find and imagine how it might be different. From this perspective the university enhances society's capacity more adequately to reflect and promote the values of democracy and social justice that are the inherent product of reasoned deliberation. For example, we might observe that those who have been fortunate enough to enter higher education in order to engage in such critical scholarship have only ever been the already relatively privileged members of an élite social group. We cannot therefore consider how access to higher education is to be widened without also considering the unequal distribution of power in societies which perpetuates such privilege. In the UK, government advisers such as Adonis (1998) have acknowledged this. Less readily considered, however, is the implication that the very concepts of academic excellence and the maintenance of standards can only be understood in a political context that addresses the unequal distribution of wealth, power and privilege in society as a whole.

These two analyses – the university that serves society, and the university as its scholarly critic – while existing in tension, are in fact both present at any one time. It takes educational imagination to work within this. As the mathematician and philosopher A N Whitehead (1929: 145) put it: 'The proper function of a university is the imaginative acquisition of knowledge . . . A university is imaginative or it is nothing – at least nothing useful.'

Learning to comply or learning to contest

The individual learner's relationship with the teacher, as well as the university's relationship with the wider society, can be viewed as a dynamic tension between compliance and contestation. To explore this, I want to consider what is taking place right here and now as I write this chapter and you read it.

Reading and writing are instances of learning and teaching. They typify what takes place in educational institutions: students learn from, amongst other things, texts that teach them. Reading this, you are performing as a learner; and I, in my authorial role, am performing as the teacher. I am attempting to engage you in a subject matter of my choosing by sharing some of my understanding, and hoping that you will gain something of value from the reading.

Now as I write this, I wonder what you might learn from it. But since this form of communication (like the formal lecture) precludes any kind of conversation at this point, I am not able to check on how it is received. If I am successful you may avoid falling asleep and continue to the end. You may feel that you have some grasp of what I am trying to say and may remember the gist of the chapter. If I do a really good job, I may altogether engage you and you may feel you have a clear idea of what I want to communicate. In that case, you will have complied with my expectations about what I had to write (or teach), and both my performance as a writer (teacher), and yours as a reader (learner), will have conformed to the best predictions regarding its outcome. And, in principle, this chapter – in traditional old-fashioned textbook style – could be followed by a test to check up that all had gone according to plan.

Such an account of reading and writing has been likened to the passing of a message from the full vessel of the author/teacher to the empty vessel of the reader/student (Readings 1996). Or, like Freire 1970 we might use the metaphor of banking and building capital to describe what the learner does with the resulting knowledge.

A more enlightened view of the nature of writing and reading – or teaching and learning – takes the reader's contribution into account. For example, you may feel either that what I communicate sheds light upon your experience, or that it is incomplete or conflicts with it. It may be that you believe my account is imbued with values which you share. Or you may feel that my whole argument is flawed by an illogical sequence of ideas, or even that I am misusing language. You may, after reading the chapter, reflect further on some of the things I have written. You may even want to reconsider your past experience and come to see it a little differently in the light of your reading, or you may compare my ideas with others you have heard or read about or with the ideas of friends. Indeed, with all this going on, your *interpretation*, or *reading*, of what I have to say will be different from the next person's.

This second account gives life to the reader (learner) as an active participant. As Barthes put it, this 'birth of the reader must be at the cost of the death of the author' (1977). This might seem a somewhat dramatic way of envisaging *my* future! But it highlights the way in which readers (or the audience of a lecture or the members of a facilitated group discussion) create their own meanings. These are constructed, or reconstructed, from the text without access to the author's supposed intended outcomes.

Such an approach to reading this chapter presupposes an engagement that is active, critical, reflective and imaginative. The author's contribution is acknowledged to be open to question, contestable, and open to different interpretations. For that reason, it will be very difficult, if not impossible, to predict in any detail what you will have learnt. No simple end-of-chapter test is likely to shed much light on the complexity of your thoughts, reflections, feelings and imaginings. And to make matters worse – worse, that is, as far as our ability to assess this educational experience goes – it may be that some of your reflections are further reflected upon at some point in the future. Perhaps there emerges a train of thinking which continues long after you have forgotten all about reading this. But you won't know about that until it happens, and may even then be unaware of the links.

In my first account of reading this chapter, the assumption was that ideally the reading should conform to the author's intentions. In the second account, the reading is assumed to be critical, contestational and imaginative. This argument, however, can be extended to apply to any form of learning interaction. Lectures, group discussions, computer-mediated communications, and so on, can all be viewed as texts which are intended to lead to certain prescribed outcomes, or alternatively, that learners construct and reconstruct these texts in the light of their critical 'readings'.

Thus there are two ways of thinking about learners and the teacher, just as there are two ways of thinking about the university and society. The first account privileges compliance, predictability and control; the second, contestation, novelty and freedom.

If universities are to provide a critical as well as a compliant function in relation to society, then we must acknowledge the extent to which learning is not an altogether predictable activity. Learning is a bit of a risky business. Perhaps that is why Confucius said that it was a vexatious and anxious one.

Recent developments in the light of this dynamic

The dominant public discourse on learning can be viewed in relation to this dynamic. For example, in the UK the (then) Minister of State for Higher Education said, at a public lecture, that the major function of the university, as far as teaching was concerned, was to meet the skill shortage in the global market-place (Blackstone 2000). Such a view was not contestable. It was stated as a matter of fact and was presumed to be common sense. It portrayed the university as providing a compliant service to the market. Tessa Blackstone was not suggesting that the imperatives of the market-place might be questioned by scholarly investigation, not envisaging that the university might question the relationships of power between the rich and poor within which the markets operate; she was not suggesting that the university might be concerned about the interests served by the global market-place and how they might impact upon social justice. Her assumption – a political assumption taken to be common sense – was that the market will and should be in control, and that the universities will comply by providing the services demanded of them. Many commentators, such as Friedman (2000), support this view of globalisation as being an irresistible and transformative power, transforming education just as it transforms other social institutions and practices.

This one-way transaction between education and society mirrors a one-way transaction between learner and teacher. For here we find a similar relationship of compliance and conformity that is assumed to be desirable. The subsequent UK Minister of State for Higher Education, speaking about her time as a student at university, said in her first interview with the press (Hodge 2001) that she recollected that she had done very little work when she studied at university some thirty years earlier. She only got a third class degree. 'I should have been *forced* to do more work,' she said, 'it was outrageous.'

No doubt the Minister should have done more work, but she is here holding her teachers, rather than herself, responsible for her short-comings. Again we can see the implication that the teacher should force compliance upon the student, whose response should be one of servility and conformity to expectations. In her view, responsibility for learning (or lack of it, in her case) lies with the teacher not the learner.

These two examples illustrate the emphasis that is placed, throughout the global economy, upon a compliant relationship between higher education and society, and between students and their teachers. At the same time, various central initiatives in the UK and elsewhere have encouraged academics to think more seriously about how students evaluate the teaching they receive. Funding has been made available to encourage the development of innovative approaches to teaching, and to explore the potential of new technologies. Programmes of work for students now offer them greater choice of subjects. Additional forms of support for students have been developed to improve their ability to study. Students have been encouraged to develop skills, rather than solely academic knowledge. They have been encouraged to become more active learners, to reflect upon their own learning, and to take responsibility for it, rather than respond passively. There has been a shift from an emphasis upon teaching towards an emphasis on learning. With their differences in interests, abilities and backgrounds, students have been put in the centre stage of academic work.

Such changes would appear to acknowledge the more imaginative aspects of learning and to support critical scholarship – and not just conformity and compliance – amongst students. When we take the wider political context into account, however, a rather different picture emerges. In the UK, 37 per cent less was spent on educating each university student in the year 2000 than was the case in 1980 (Livingstone 2001). At the same time, measures have been devised for ensuring – or assuring – that teaching and learning is effective and that the reduced resources from the public purse are well spent. Consequently, a bureaucratic account of learning has emerged in order to quantify and compare the performance of institutions by making supposedly objective assessments of effectiveness.

My first accounts of reading this chapter, in which I suggested that the reader might learn what I intended, was easy to assess. The second, in which I speculated about the variety of ways in which the reader might respond, was difficult to assess with any accuracy. The need to provide objective, numerical assessments of the effectiveness of teaching or learning inevitably prioritises the former way of looking at learning as a predictable and limited activity. Under this regime, teaching is presumed to consist in the *delivery* of a text that is presumed to be transparent.

Understandably, if we want to ensure value for money, we need to be able to predict and measure. The fact that learning – or at least the more imaginative or critical aspects of learning – does not so readily submit to prediction and measurement is unfortunate!

This prioritising of conformity and predictability impacts upon how courses are planned, upon the way students are taught, and upon the way learning and teaching are evaluated. For example, when academic staff design curricula, the templates they are required to follow and questions they have to answer presuppose a particular view of the curriculum. This is a view that the curriculum has (and should have) definable outcomes, that these outcomes can be measured, and thus the effectiveness of provision assessed. Lecturers have to assume that they should be able to give a measurable account of what the student is intended to come out with. While this might be possible as far as the author's or the teacher's *intentions* are concerned, such intentions take little account of the unpredictable, long term, and individual response of the reader or learner.

Scholarly work has been described as the struggle 'to produce out of the chaos of the human experience some grain of order won by the intellect.' (Annan 1999: 53). Such intellectual struggle cannot be reduced to predictable outcomes, however politically and administratively convenient this might be. Much research through the 1960s, 1970s and 1980s in the school sector demonstrated that a curriculum is a much more complex and unpredictable affair, much more like my second account of this chapter: more dependent upon what the learner contributes to the process. Such a view of the curriculum was perhaps best articulated by Stenhouse (1975) as a basis for curriculum research and development. Scholarly work – whether we are talking about academic research or student learning – is after all a form of enquiry, and an essential feature of any enquiry is that you don't know the outcome before you start!

So whilst many of these recent developments have been designed to shed more light on students' learning and recognise its diverse and creative nature, a regime of audit and accountability has emerged which seriously undermines this intended effect. It is a form of reductionism that trivialises the richness of human experience.

The changing disciplines

So far I have presented a somewhat gloomy picture of compliance. I now look more optimistically at the disciplines and interdisciplinary work and how recent developments here might support a more lively culture of contestation.

It has been claimed that academics often join their profession because of their love of teaching (Boyer 1990). Many studies, however, particularly from the kinds of institutions described as 'research led', suggest that most identify themselves primarily in terms of their discipline (Squires 1987, Rowland 2000). Academics tend to see themselves as, for example, historians or engineers who teach – and indeed often enjoy teaching – rather than primarily as teachers who have history or engineering as their subject.

A discipline is not simply a body of knowledge but a way of coming to know. It describes the field of chaos out of which, to use Annan's words, we struggle to produce 'some grain of order won by the intellect.' It also shapes the kind of order students and researchers create and the ways they carry out the struggle.

Different disciplines involve different priorities about their purposes, different kinds of questions and different ways of answering them. An engineer, an architect and an ecologist might have very different ideas about what constitutes a good bridge, or an appropriate bridge in a particular situation. Thus we might say that from an engineering point of view, or from an ecological point of view, this or that is a preferable design. Similarly, a sociologist and a historian are likely to have different ideas about the significance of a painting, and different, again, from the viewpoint of an art critic.

During the last thirty years or so the disciplines have undergone radical changes as a result of two developments. First, there has been a rapid increase in the rate at which knowledge – or at least accounts of knowledge – has increased. During the 1990s the world-wide literature in the field of chemistry, for example, grew by more than half a million articles per year. At that rate, four full time research assistants would be needed merely to read the *titles* of chemistry articles as they are produced. In the sciences, 8,500 different specialities were recently identified (Clark 2000). Secondly, research and teaching has been more geared towards serving the economy. Such practical or commercial needs invariably require knowledge from different disciplines. Providing water in an undeveloped region, for example, requires sociological and ecological knowledge – and probably political and botanical knowledge – as well as engineering.

This rapid expansion of knowledge, together with the emphasis on the profitable purposes to which it might be put, has led to the emergence of new disciplines, new combinations of discipline, challenges to existing disciplinary boundaries and the emergence of a field of studies devoted to the study of disciplinarity (Messer-Davidow 1993). It has impacted directly on research and on the courses we offer students.

One result of this has been the modularization of the curriculum, in which courses of study have, in many places, been split into fragments, enabling hybrid courses to be constructed by students selecting different modules from different disciplines or fields of study. While it has been argued that this gives students greater freedom of choice and enables courses to be constructed flexibly to suit the needs of the market, such freedom comes at a cost. The cost is often the lack of coherence of courses of study, with consequent shallowness of learning and inadequate opportunity for students to get to grips with any particular discipline (Winter 1996). In such a context, learners are treated as consumers in a supermarket, picking and mixing educational commodities with little sense of continuation and development. Often called 'multidisciplinary', such courses are often, in fact, non-disciplinary since the depth of study is insufficient to enable learners to engage with the critical approaches, values and paradigms of any particular discipline.

While a broad range of studies – as in the USA's liberal arts degrees – can be a valuable tertiary education, the greatest value of working across different disciplines is only achieved when learners (as students or researchers) begin to grapple with the contesting and often conflicting values, purposes and approaches that underlie different disciplines. This is a process of critical reflection upon knowledge. It has been argued that such critical reflection should be at the heart of what is meant by a higher education (Barnett 1997). Interdisciplinarity is this contestational approach to work across disciplinary boundaries.

Interdisciplinarity and contestation

Disciplines thrive on informed contestation. Einstein's work on the development of physics, for example, challenged taken for granted mathematical models used to investigate the physical world. This influenced philosophical perspectives about the nature of reality. His ideas about the relativity of space-time, although rooted in the physical sciences, contributed to more relativistic ways of thinking in the humanities and social sciences. The appropriateness of this transfer of ideas from one field into another has been widely contested.

Challenges to disciplines often emerge when metaphors and images that underpin them are adopted by other disciplines. In chaos theory (Prigogine and Stengers 1985, Gleick 1988), for example, research initially conducted in order to try to predict the ways in which the flow of fluids varies with temperature (an important thing to understand if you are a meteorologist) led to very general ideas about the relationships between states of chaos and states of order. Some of the scientists who worked in that field later employed their ideas and theories in an attempt to understand how predictions might be made concerning the sometimes orderly, and sometimes chaotic, behaviour of share prices and stock markets.

Later, ideas from chaos theory were taken up in the field of management and economics – with titles such as *Chaos, Management and Economics* (Parker and Stacey 1994) – and in the field of Curriculum Studies (Green and Bigum 1990). The notion of chaos has now become the jargon of a clique of management gurus with even the unpredictable workings of Osama Bin Laden and the al-Qaida claimed by some to be analysable in terms of such ideas (Meek 2001).

Theories derived from one context of knowledge cannot, however, simply be transferred into another. It is a process which, fired by curiosity, should be at once rigorously disciplined, and also imaginatively playful.

Children are, of course, specialists when it comes to the playful transfer of ideas across fields of experience. Studies of the primary school classroom (Armstrong 1980, Rowland 1984) illuminate the delight of young children discovering, for example, how such dry things as multiplication tables can be represented by satisfying patterns, and later, that interesting shapes and patterns can be understood in terms of numbers. Such 'play' – for that is often how it is experienced – can give new meaning to how children understand numbers and design, and the relationship between these two initially different areas of their experience. Such creative leaps of imagination are as important, though perhaps much more difficult, in the learning of the university researcher as they are in the learning of the young child.

Interdisciplinary learning and research also offers the possibility of contesting conceptions of identity and professional role. For example, in the UK, stimulated by the interests of the previous Chief Medical Officer (Calman 2000: xiv), and drawing upon experience in the USA, there has been a recent development of a field called medical humanities. One might suppose medicine to involve humanistic as well as scientific understanding since it involves the application of science to the human condition. Recently, however, the President of the General Medical Council in UK accused his own profession of expressing a culture based upon a narrowly scientific outlook towards patient care (Irvine 2001). The field of medical humanities can be seen as an attempt to correct such a narrowly scientific bias.

The exciting interdisciplinary possibility here is that insights from the humanities will contest accepted norms in medical practice, and that the realities and demands of medicine and health care will produce new insights in these humanities. In the process, the very idea of what it is to be a doctor on the one hand, or an artist or poet on the other, will be informed by an engagement between humanistic and scientific forms of enquiry. Such a development involves argument and contestation as the presumptions and practices in the different fields confront each other. Such contestation would contribute to growth in both the disciplines of medicine and the humanities.

Conclusions

For this interdisciplinary approach to fulfil its potential – with the consequent intellectual challenges for students and academic staff – opportunities need to be provided for students and staff to meet and engage with each other across disciplinary boundaries. Spaces have to be created where uncomfortable questions can be asked and tentative ideas explored without the continual fear of failure that often dominates academic life. One of the major roles of academic or educational development can be seen as being to provide such intellectual spaces (Rowland 2002). There needs to be a real engagement with the intellectual work of teaching and research. It is not sufficient for staff to meet merely in order to manage procedures, or students to engage with one area of study after another without exploring the conflicts and differences between them. But teaching and learning, like research, must be focused on and motivated by a passion for the subject. Without this, contestation is trivial. In the current climate of accountability and risk aversion, words like 'passion' and 'love of the subject' never figure in the prescriptions and requirements of central agencies with their focus upon developing skills, gaining qualifications and maintaining standards.

Interdisciplinary work offers the potential for contestation to play a more prominent part in learning for both students and staff. It can provide an antidote to the culture of compliance that currently predominates. It requires, however, that we have the confidence to step outside our disciplinary boundaries, not leaving that disciplinary identity behind but being prepared to engage in a scholarly way with colleagues and students (and indeed the wider public) who may not share our priorities, assumptions or our specialised languages. To put it another way, academic 'tribalism' (Becher 1989) must become more 'multicultural'.

Interdisciplinary engagement of this sort, with its conflicting values and priorities, can feel unpredictable as the existing assumptions of one discipline are challenged by those of another. This unpredictability – like the unpredictability of what the reader might learn from the author's text – is an essential feature of enquiry, research and education. In a society which has become increasingly unpredictable, it is important that those who teach, as well as their students, acknowledge their inability predict the outcome of the search for knowledge, rather than pretend that learning can be reduced to the predictable.

Higher education is moving into a new set of relationships with the wider social and economic world. As a consequence, exciting possibilities are emerging, and attention is increasingly being focused upon the contribution that learning and research can make to the wider community. In the process, however, ways must be found to create and protect the space to stimulate debate, contestation and imagination amongst students, staff and the wider community. These are as necessary conditions of higher education as they are of democracy itself. The struggle to create these kinds of spaces is a form of resistance in the face of the forces of compliance. To promote them is, as Confucius put it, a 'vexatious and anxious task.'

3

New Labour, New Professionalism

DENNIS HAYES

Dennis Hayes is impatient with the notion of the learner as patient. He argues that learners are being forced into the recovery position, in which they can be cared for so long as they lie still, quietly being understood by their educators, whose role has come to be seen as therapeutic. This way, he argues, no one learns anything beyond their helpless dependency on the caring educator. Hayes' critique is further developed by Colley; his tone is direct and down-to-earth, preparing for the discussion by Burn and Finnigan and by Satterthwaite of the wrapping-up of meaning in academy-speak.

The argument I put forward in this chapter is that a new form of professionalism is gaining ground in post-compulsory education (PCE), one that has adopted a *therapeutic ethos*. The consequence of this will be the increasing use of therapeutic language and methods in teaching that will dissipate student potential in a way that is neither beneficial to society nor to the achievement of the educational ambitions of individual students.

We are moving towards the creation of what I want to call the 'therapeutic college' that will close the gap between the 'therapeutic school' (Nolan 1998), and what I have labelled the 'therapeutic university' (Hayes 2002; Hayes 2003; Hayes and Wynyard 2002a and 2002b). The therapeutic ethos has developed late in PCE because of its neglect by government and the strong links the sector traditionally had with the world of work. This economic nexus gave it a temporary and seeming independence that fostered in professional minds the illusion of critical space that could be used to promote social or economic well-being. This illusion may actually speed up the transformation of post-compulsory educators into therapists.

One clearly therapeutic impulse, the idea of PCE as transformative through the development of the democratic forms of communication, comes from seemingly 'radical' PCE educators and the thinkers they draw upon. These are the 'critical theorists', in particular, Jürgen Habermas, who provide a theoretical base for this approach. As we shall see, Habermas' radicalism turns out to be no more than a self-reflective form of therapeutic communication that appeals to and flatters PCE educators today.

To understand how this therapeutic ethos has begun to dominate PCE thought it is useful to put it in the contemporary British context. There are two important developments that readers unfamiliar with the British educational system may not have encountered (see Armitage *et al* 2003, chapters 1 and 9, for a fuller explanation). These are, firstly, a change in direction of Government policy from promoting particular vocational and training initiatives to a concern with the whole curriculum on offer in the Further Education (FE) Colleges. Secondly, and as a consequence of this, there is a desire on the part of Government to ensure that all FE lecturers are qualified teachers to enable them to meet the challenges of this new curriculum. This is the context in which the Government and PCE educators have begun to re-examine the idea of professionalism. It will be useful, therefore, to begin with the New Labour Government's renewed interest in professionalism.

New Labour's Professional Turn

Estelle Morris, when she was Secretary of State for Education and Skills, defined the contemporary problem of professionalism from the viewpoint of New Labour's nervous political élite:

> Gone are the days when doctors and teachers could say, with a straight face, 'trust me, I'm a professional'. So we need to be clear about what does constitute professionalism for the modern world. And what will provide the basis for a fruitful and new era of trust between Government and the teaching profession. This is an arena ripe for debate and we welcome views from all round the education

system and from others, including parents and business people. (Morris 2001: 19)

All the key aspects of New Labour's attitude to professionalism are expressed in this quotation from the aptly titled *Professionalism and Trust*. Firstly, there is the scathing rejection of the teacher as an autonomous expert. Secondly, there is an abstract semantic search for the meaning of trust – something that must follow once the autonomy that is of the essence of trust has been rejected. Finally, we get an elevation of 'others' – 'stakeholders' or more properly 'know-nothings' to the role of experts in a search for meaning. Out of such confusion comes the therapeutic urge to enable us to cope with the loss of meaning.

New Labour is only categorical about what is *not* appropriate in the development of this new professionalism:

> It is important to trust our professionals to get on with the job. That does not mean leaving professionals to go their own way, without scrutiny – we will always need the constant focus on effective teaching and learning, and the accountability measures described above. But what it does mean is that we shall increasingly want to see professionals at the core, to join us in shaping the patterns for the schools of the future. (Morris 2001: 26)

Here we have the 'Millennium Dome' or 'big tent' view of profession-alism. As long as you are on the inside of the dome/tent that is O.K. but you cannot have any independent thought or autonomy. This atti-tude does not imply any confidence in professionals and is merely an expression of anxious authoritarianism.

Why raise the issue of creating a 'modern' professionalism at all when you have no confidence in professionals? The obvious reason is New Labour's simple desire to get people on side. In Anthony Seldon's monumental tome *The Blair Effect*, he concludes that 'The Net Blair Effect' is a matter of style. New Labour has lost its traditional work-ing class base and has 'reached out as never before to embrace the establishment, including the City, business, the professions, the media and the Church of England, and even independent schools' (Seldon 2001: 594). Denis Kavanagh, in the same volume, adds 'South East England' to this list (Kavanagh 2001: 16). Trying to get professionals on side is clearly one of the major motivations behind New Labour policy.

The need to get people on side explains, in part, constant changes of policy. Alan Smithers has commented that New Labour in its educational thinking 'desperately wanted to be seen to be doing good things' to the extent that 'Every day without a new education headline was regarded as a day wasted . . .'. And he asks, 'What are we to make of all this activity? Has the Blair government really had 'a big picture', with the many initiatives necessitated by numerous faults in the system? Or has it tended to dissipate its political capital by failing to focus sufficiently on the main issues, rushing off in all directions?' (Smithers 2001: 425). Hodgson and Spours are more certain. In their well-known study of New Labour's education policy, they state that 'New Labour does not appear to know what kind of direction it wants the education and training system to follow' (1999: 145).

But these responses simply miss the point. It is true that in one sense New Labour does not know what it is doing, but these changes are not about solving problems or promoting any sort of 'big' educational idea. They are experiments in trying to win over a new audience. This narrowly functional approach to policy is of the greatest importance as New Labour has lost its traditional electoral constituency. It seems impossible for New Labour to identify any clear constituency at all. Any policy will be tried if it looks like reaching an audience that might support the Government, and even vote for it when necessary.

This turn towards a new constituency is only one aspect of the new interest in professionalism; as we shall see, there is a more profound disconnection behind the superficial and the vote-winning.

Professionalism's 'Three Ways'

To properly understand the contemporary concern with professionalism requires a political rather than a philosophical analysis, although, in the current period, the issue often takes an epistemological and, hence, philosophical form. In PCE literature the topic of professionalism was previously entirely neglected (see Minton 1991 and Walklin 1990). Recently, we can find a minimalist definition of professionalism as merely keeping up with developments and keeping subject knowledge up-to-date, alongside confused discussions of the multiple meanings of professionalism (Huddleston and Unwin 1997: 149). Alternatively, we are presented with descriptions of a 'professional crisis' involving a struggle against the de-professionalisation or proletarianisation of PCE educators (Robson 2000). Similarly, managerialism and bureaucratisation are described as the cause of this de-professionalisation (Avis 1995). Some serious philosophical analyses discuss the criteria for professionalism but do not address the contemporary political context (Carr 2000). But it was Donald Schön who came closest to the heart of the contemporary debate when he discussed the issue as 'a crisis of confidence in professional knowledge', because 'Professionals have been disturbed to find that they cannot account for processes they have come to see as central to professional competence . . .' (Schön 1983: 19).

Despite his identifying a deep crisis of epistemological faith, Schön's solution is to introduce the notion of reflection in action; and the rest is a well-known story. However, Schön merely substitutes the real problem of the lack of faith in what he describes as 'positivisitic/scientific' knowledge, with a metaphysical defence of professional practice. This avoids the issue that disturbed educators in the 1980s and now.

What I want to identify here is the trajectory of PCE professionalism in the context of some theoretical discussion, a lot of policy making and a few practical ideas that are best understood through the concept of the politics of the 'third way'. To talk meaningfully of the politics of the 'third way', however, requires some understanding of the 'second' and 'first' ways (see Blair 1998; Giddens 1998; Hayes and Hudson 2001; Armitage *et al* 2003 Ch.9).

The first way, as an historical period, ran from the time of post-war reconstruction until the middle of the 1970s. Throughout this time the idea of professionalism was based on a PCE educator's or a teacher's independence and autonomy in all areas of their work because of their (subject) knowledge. It is important to understand that this consensus about professional autonomy was an accidental feature of an historical period. It was not worked out from an epistemological or philosophical position. This explains in part why the educational thinkers we associate with this period – such as Paul Hirst – have moved with the times and changed or abandoned their views. What made the first way unique was the post-war boom. That allowed the expansion of education and the luxury of disinterested inquiry for a short time even if it never really amounted to a golden age (see Hayes 2002).

The end of the post war boom and the start of the 'second way' can be dated, for our purposes, from 1976 when Callaghan's 'great debate' marked the end of consensus and opened education up to market forces. The second way is characterised by the Thatcherite project to destroy 'socialism', that is, trade unions and the institutions and communities of the period of welfare consensus. However, Thatcherism was an entirely destructive project that left nothing in their place except illusory 'market mechanisms' imposed on all public sector institutions, including schools, colleges and universities. The legacy of the 'second way' is a morass of managerialist and bureaucratic practices experienced by PCE educators and others as constituting de-professionalisation.

And so to the third way, in which no return to the welfare consensus seems possible, and the market is equally unacceptable. In these circumstances what characterises the third way is the artificiality and fragility of all policies and practices. Discussions of education and teaching – including most of the contributions to this book – do not set themselves in the context of third way politics. This is unfortunate because the politics of the third way arise within the unique historical moment in which we live. The third way period can be dated from 1989 when the collapse of communism, as the seeming alternative to capitalism, brought to an end a period of history that had run for two hundred years since the great French Revolution of 1789. Politics as we knew it ended at this time, and, more importantly, the historical subject that drove society forward, what we used to call the working class, was simply absent in any institutional or organisational form. The consequence of this is uncertainty and constant change. Policy-makers find their projects fragile because they are not argued for or directed at any community, as traditional communities and their institutions no longer exist.

This political climate of the third way is, therefore, fundamentally about the uncertainties of a political elite anxious about ordinary people. This is the more profound disconnection. Lacking traditional organisations that represent, and also discipline, people, the political élite can only encourage low horizons and low expectations. For purposes closely related to their own need for reassurance, they promote ideas and policies that lead to self-limitation and self-regulation. Some of these policies are discussed below.

The attitude of the political élite to professionalism over the period of the three ways can be seen to move from a consensus about independence, to seeking control through the market, to fostering forms of self-regulation that are open to a therapeutic orientation. This has an epistemological parallel in the shift from (subject) knowledge to (therapeutic) process.

Therapeutic Policy-Making

New Labour is slowly developing policies that provide clear evidence of what I am identifying as a *therapeutic turn*. I will illustrate this with reference to some key recent initiatives, before showing how they are rooted in the theoretical outpourings of a retreating political left and their fellow travellers in the world of educational theory. This radical backing has the possibility of providing a basis for some sustained and consistent therapeutic policy-making that will win professional support. However, the consequences of this radicalism are worse than being subject to the vacillations of the third way.

Connexions is the policy initiative that provides the strongest evidence of therapeutic policy-making that results from the anxiety about ordinary people. There are something like 1,231,000 *therapeutic* workers in Britain today. This is a grand total that includes guidance workers, mediators, counsellors (632,000) and therapists (Heartfield 2002: 236). This already makes it seem that people cannot deal with life's vicissitudes without guidance from experts. The core of the *Connexions* strategy is to increase the number of therapeutic workers dramatically by giving every young person a 'personal advisor' (PA) to guide them through education and into adult life. Social workers, youth and community workers, careers and guidance workers are all being retrained or re-designated as PAs. The focus of the PA's work derives from the more therapeutic aspects of guidance that now exist, effectively adopting a practice that assumes that every young person has special needs. This means that they cannot be left to grow up as they did in the past, but now need to be guided towards adult life by state-trained advisors.

To a lesser extent the innovations of *Curriculum 2000* expressed a similar move towards a guidance approach by introducing Individual Learning Plans, personal tutorials and the 'working with others' element of key skills. The individualised curriculum envisioned in the new Green Paper on 14–19 Education, *Extending Opportunities, Raising Standards,* will enhance this.

Citizenship education would be another area in which a therapeutic ethos could be promoted, but as Karen Evans has complained 'learning for citizenship is almost invisible in Post-16 education (Evans 2000: 157). We can predict that it will be a major area of the developing 14–19 curriculum package. Citizenship education will become popular with PCE educators, as it is with teachers, because it seems to be a genuine attempt to motivate young people to be active in the community. But this attempt will necessarily fail, because it is part of the negative achievement of Thatcherism that traditional communities have disappeared. There is no community to be active in, which reflects the accuracy of Mrs Thatcher's claim, made in *Women's Own* in 1987, that 'There is no such thing as society, only individuals and their families'. The end result of citizenship education in this context will be therapeutic as it can only encourage empathy towards others (social inclusion) and involvement in forms of therapeutic support for the disadvantaged.

However, it is in teacher training that we find the therapeutic ethos at its strongest. Although the debate about the negative impact of competence-based education and training (CBET) has been dominant in teacher education theory for some time, Usher and Edwards have pointed out that the introduction of competencies is paradoxical. The commodification and control of knowledge that is the political purpose of the introduction of CBET, exists alongside a humanistic approach to teaching and, we may add, to teacher education. Usher and Edwards have made the point that the notion of competence is: 'cast in behavioural terms but the discourse is itself not behaviourist. It is precisely because it is not, but rather interwoven with liberal humanist discourse, that it is powerful' (1994: 110). They add that: 'In its liberal humanist form, competence is more a form of 'seduction' than oppression' (1994: 111). CEBT is, in fact, largely delivered using humanistic methods and this is a device to make the approach acceptable. What Usher and Edwards see as humanistic, I would call *therapeutic*. The humanistic or subject-based liberal educational curriculum would be impossible to deliver through CBET. What *does* complement CBET is the therapeutic curriculum, the concern with personal development and the growth of self-aware-ness and understanding (reflective practice). The influence of John Dewey may be of some importance here (Carr 1995; Nolan 1998; Harkin *et al* 2000). However, the appearance of Carl Rogers' work on the reading lists for the PGCE/Cert. Ed in PCE – evidenced by course handbooks – is not just an indication of his influence on teacher-educators, but also an expression of an explicitly therapeutic turn. This therapeutic turn is given more emphasis and support by radical writers on education who influence teacher educators, or who are teacher educators themselves.

Therapeutic Theory

My first example of therapeutic theory is taken from a popular intro-ductory textbook for intending teachers and teacher educators as well as a wider audience, *Professional Issues for Teachers and Student Teachers* edited by Mike Cole of the Hillcole Group of socialist aca-demics. This short work supports a radical agenda for professionals working in all areas of education. Cole argues that New Labour's educational project may seek to reject the excesses of Thatcherism but 'the organising principle for New Labour, as it was for its prede-cessors in government, is economic effectiveness' (Cole 1999: x). Cole wants to set the attempt to improve standards within a different agenda that emphasises equality. The way forward for progressive educators is for equality and equal opportunity issues to 'command a much higher profile' (p110). This is the familiar agenda of radical educators. However, an important development appears in one of Cole's contributor's discussion of bullying:

> Real progress for education can only be made by longer-term investment in the foundations of the education system: in building the self-esteem of *all* our children. Pastoral care policies and the building of a positive whole-school culture should be at the *heart* of

our education system, not a disposable add-on. Any attempt to improve the health of our schools that does not focus fundamentally on the heart [sic] will ultimately be doomed to failure. Pastoral care systems are the way we enable our children to become more human. They must be allowed to work. (Parker 1999: 83)

This emphasis on self-esteem as being at the heart of a humanistic education project is an unusually clear description of the therapeutic school. The same arguments can be applied to the FE college.

My second example shows the influence of a watered-down form of Deweyian pragmatism that is, in the end, also a sort of therapy. Harkin, Turner and Dawn argue that 'Much of what passes for education is dull and of little relevance to learners' (Harkin *et al* 2000: 140), and add:

It is time to build a high-trust, democratic education system that respects learners and their experiences, listens closely to their expressions of interest and need, builds partnerships between teachers, learners, parents, the community, and employers so that young adults learn what they wish to learn, and how they wish to learn. (p140)

The language here, 'trust' 'partnership' and 'respect' for 'learners and their experiences', is that of the therapist rather than the educationalist. Despite this language, Harkin *et al* believe that the new cohorts of students, now condemned to education or training, rather than being properly employed, may be, if we only see them as such, a real asset:

. . . the catalyst for fundamental change in education. Not content to receive more of what they have already endured with indifference or hostility, they may challenge educationalists to provide an experience which promotes rational autonomy, personal engagement and a healthy social democracy. (p141)

This somewhat quixotic vision of the potential of PCE throws in every social hope that disillusioned educators might have in these disconnected times. How real are these hopes? The specific condition of their achievement is that 'we', the educators and educational institutions, should value and accept these new students and their experiences. This is a therapeutic rather than a radical approach.

The assumption made by Harkin *et al* of the transformative potential of working class students is false. Even if such potential existed, it would be diluted and displaced by the navel-gazing forms of therapy disguised as education that they propose.

The third example of what should be seen as therapeutic theory for the new therapeutic professionalism is from post-modern thinkers, who reject the possibility of knowledge (Foucault 1973). The Enlightenment philosophers, Newton, Locke, Pascal, Descartes and others, established the modern intellectual values of confidence in knowledge, objective truth, reason, science, progress and experimentation. They argued that these values were the basis for the ability of mankind to control, rather than be subject to, nature. The student rebellions and the *évènements* of 1968 were clearly expressions of this belief in human progress. They could hardly be otherwise at the time of the space race and the first moon landing. However, the influence of Stalinism on politics at that time meant that the locus for social change in the minds of youthful radical students and lecturers had shifted. It was no longer in the workplace and with the working class, but in the university with radical middle class students. This was another act in a long period of political retreat by radicals who had no connection with workers and were appalled by Stalinist politics, and became isolated outside of the political organisations of the official Communist Parties.

This retreat has now gone further than ever before with attacks by postmodernists on confidence in the objectivity of knowledge (Usher and Edwards 1994) and to some extent by seemingly radical thinkers (Bloomer 1996; Bloomer 1997; Harkin *et al* 2001). Postmodernists ask, 'whose knowledge?', and stress the variety and relativity of truth and distrust reason. More specifically, they distrust science and the very idea of progress, which leads them to emphasise what they see as the damage done by attempting to control nature. They also emphasise different and particular views rather than universal theories which attempt to explain how the world or society works. Such views are often consciously playful and because of this they are therapeutic. Postmodernism is fun, amusing, full of insights, but ultimately just a reflection of anxious times rather than a serious contribution to educational thought. Fortunately, postmodernist thought has had little impact on the PCE sector, other than, and most worryingly, in some sectors of HE.

This is not the case with the fourth example of therapeutic theory that is becoming influential: the school of thought that stems from the work of Jürgen Habermas, a philosopher linked with the neo-Marxist Frankfurt School (Habermas 1974 and 1984; Therborn 1978).

From Habermas we get two general ideas that are applied to PCE. The first is a search for a 'communication free of domination' (see Therborn 1978: 137–9). Using this notion some writers have commented that in PCE institutions 'it is clear that we are far from establishing an ideal speech community but importantly we should be endeavouring to make classrooms more open in language practices'. They explain that 'Differences of gender, culture and outlook should be celebrated as part of a democratic endeavour' (Harkin *et al* 2001: 135).

What is absurd about such views of the potential radicalism of PCE and of its students (see Harkin *et al* 2001: 141), is that they re-locate power struggles in the real world to talk in the classroom. This is a comfortable verbal radicalism without any social consequences. We can make this point clearer by considering the second idea, of praxis, often associated with Habermas (Habermas 1974), though the philosophical originator is Aristotle. The idea of praxis may be approached in various ways, but it is best understood as a political rather than an academic concept. The notion of praxis was originally part of the political vocabulary of German and Italian Marxist political thinking. In this context it described the process by which a revolutionary party tested its theoretical ideas and developed its theory through engagement in the class struggle. There is a long tradition of writing that stresses that only through working class political organisation can spontaneous individual consciousness be transcended (see Lukács 1922/1971). Habermas is conscious of this and declares, '. . . I do not pose the question of organisation, and thus do not draw the consequences of knowledge directed towards liberation . . .' (1974: 15). The political retreat evident here is taken a step further in talking of 'praxis' as applied to isolated individuals or to teaching students in PCE.

Martin Bloomer has tried to develop a notion of studenthood that works towards placing students in the position of a potentially radical group testing themselves against their experience of PCE. He notes that 'studenthood' is often seen as a way in which students can begin to learn independently and to recognise 'the problematic nature of knowledge' (Bloomer 1996: 140). He goes further, using the term in a broader sense in which the student can 'exert influence over the curriculum' in 'the creation and confirmation of their own personal learning careers' (p140). Yet Bloomer's seemingly dynamic descriptions of PCE teaching situations, that might be an example of praxis at least in the degenerated form of 'practical wisdom' achieved through the liberation of Habermas' emancipatory interest (p160), are unlikely to result in anything but the celebration of personal experience.

The consequence of this approach will be identical to the consequence of Habermas' thought, a critical self-reflection that is a sort of therapy (see Therborn 1978: 125–128). Habermas calls this process 'therapeutic discourse' (1984: 21). The appeal of this sort of philosophy to professionals is, in fact, a false ideological sense of themselves as radicals. It relocates political problems to the classroom and pretends that they can be overcome by 'the enlightened efforts of critical students and scholars' (Therborn 1978: 139). As Therborn puts it: 'Hence Habermas's popularity . . . He combines an apparently left-wing pedigree, conventional humanism and a notion that the basic political problems are problems of communication. The blandness of these ideas is evident' (Therborn 1978: 139). These ideas may be bland but they *do* flatter PCE educators by exaggerating the potential for social change that lies in the hands of their students.

This radical view of the potential of teachers, trainers and students has a parallel in a more conservative view of PCE. Radical teacher trainers may see education as transformative for individuals, whereas managers and government policy-makers are more likely to promote the idea that FE, in particular, can regenerate the economy. We can call this the Bilston College Fallacy, as that college did much to promote this view in a series of in-house publications. Ironically, the College went into severe financial difficulties shortly after the publication of their major book on this topic (see Reeves 1997 and Bryan 1998). Both the radical and conservative views of FE over-estimate the role of education in, respectively, politics and the economy.

Beyond the Therapeutic State

The turn towards therapy is based on the premise of low expectations. The horizons we set for ourselves and our students diminish as the social antagonism that produced big ideas such as 'socialism' are no longer in play. The absence of the working class as a political force pushing society forward leads to social atomisation and an individuation that turns towards the subjective. It culminates in a belief that improving inter-subjective communication is all that can be achieved. This explains the current vogue for Habermas' work.

A time of low horizons is a time in which we have a diminished view of the potential of people. We have discussed this as an epistemological crisis involving a rejection of the search for knowledge that is at the heart of the Enlightenment tradition. The social expression of this takes the form of a victim culture in which we see people as constantly at risk and unable to cope.

The political response to this culture, according to James L. Nolan in his seminal book *The Therapeutic State,* is that all state institutions, and education in particular, are open to the 'therapeutic ethos'. The 'therapeutic ethos' centres on building up individual self-esteem. In the face of the forces of technical rationalization it helps people cope with the effects on their private lives. It also helps people subject to racial, sexual or any other discrimination to cope with their victimhood. Like postmodernism, the therapeutic ethos is seen as oppositional:

> Though sometimes portrayed as a reaction against utilitarian capitalism, the therapeutic cultural impulse does not directly challenge or threaten the utilitarian orientation of the capitalistic order. To the contrary, the therapeutic ethic appears to complement the utilitarian ethic. It offers to soften the harshness of life in the machine without removing the machine. In fact, it is often defended as a viable source of action because of its purported efficacy. Though these two dispositions seem intuitively disparate, they may actually be complementary. (Nolan 1998: 20)

More succinctly he argues: 'The therapeutic orientation provides a personalized remedy to a highly impersonal, rationalized, bureaucratic system, but without fundamentally altering the system' (1998: 20).

What I have identified as a new professionalism based upon the therapeutic ethos is a step towards the *therapeutic college*. The prime movers in this direction will not be college authorities but PCE educators and teacher educators who have been influenced by ideas stemming from the retreat into the politics of communication that derives from Habermas' rejection of Marxism. The tragedy is that no one benefits from this development. The students attending the *therapeutic college* will be impoverished human beings taught not to seek dangerous things like knowledge and truth but more communication experiences that build up their self-esteem and that of others. PCE educators will have to engage in classes that more and more resemble circle time in the primary school. Their work will be all process and no content. Indeed, it has become popular to argue that we need an alternative conception of PCE professionalism that sees PCE educators as 'learning professionals' who will 'feel valued' (Lucas 2000: 246). The job of these new professionals will be to have a more holistic approach to their role and to develop new skills 'including offering guidance and counselling' (Lucas 2000: 244). This is an abject picture of PCE educators as learners who, just like their students, are lacking in self-esteem. This therapeutic re-professionalisation is not in the interest of PCE educators – it is something entirely demeaning.

Society will not benefit, as people educated in the therapeutic ethos to need re-assurance are not going to further the advancement of knowledge, make creative challenges or bring about developments in the economy or in social life, a life that will not be more engaging as it becomes increasingly more personal and more about the expression of feelings. A well-known proponent of the politics of the emotions is former US President Bill Clinton, the therapeutic president, whose catch phrase was 'I feel your pain' (Nolan 1998: 235–6). But empathy with people, especially cynical empathy, is no foundation for politics. A more theoretical attempt to defend such an approach is Anthony Giddens' argument for a 'democracy of the emotions' as an essential weapon 'on the front line of the struggle between cosmopolitanism and fundamentalism' (1999: 65). However, showing your feelings, expressing sympathy and crying cannot form the foundation for a new politics. No one benefits from this celebration of human frailty; we just feel more frail.

The therapeutic ethos arises out of the more negative and atomised nature of society. To go along with it is to undermine our potential to overcome individual adversity and to take control of our lives. Circle time is a poor substitute for the struggle for human achievement and social progress.

The *therapeutic college* may well be with us in the near future. Robin Wynyard, my colleague and collaborator on work exploring the *therapeutic university*, reminds me that whether or not academics bemoan the coming of these *therapeutic institutions*, students will still value the experience they have there. If that is so, it will be a triumph for the therapeutic approach in building their self-esteem. They will feel positive about what they have achieved. But their confidence will be fragile and will constantly require more therapeutic attention. This prospect is something that no one, except professional and amateur therapists, could want.

The discussions in this book are about the possible critical role of PCE and the professionals that work within it. The theme of this article is, in fact, a very old one. It is to argue that the unexamined life, the life built around improving people's self-esteem, is not worth living. The first step in ensuring that we, and our students, do not have to lead such a life is to oppose the new radical professionalism and reject the therapeutic ethos at its heart.

4

Discourse, Power and Resistance in New York: The rise of testing and accountability and the decline of teacher professionalism and local control

DAVID HURSH

David Hursh echoes Atkinson's resistance to the rhetoric of standards and accountability which pervades current education policy, and analyses high stakes testing in New York as a form of governmentality. Hursh refuses to accept the policy-makers' appeals to the rationales of economic productivity, fairness and objectivity: his analysis of the persuasive force of discourse is a theme revisited by Colley, while his call for recognition of non-dominant forms of teaching, learning and assessment is echoed in the chapters by Burn and Finnigan and Nichols.

Introduction

In this chapter, I focus on the rise of high-stakes exams in New York to address the following question: given that the introduction of high-stakes testing has had a negative effect on teachers and students by narrowing the curriculum and increasing the number of students dropping out and teachers leaving schools, how is it that these tests have received such widespread support and so little public resistance? To answer the question, I examine the ways in which New York's politicians and educational bureaucrats have used the discourses of fairness, objectivity, and an implicit neo-liberal economic rationale to convince the public of the need for testing and accountability systems. My analysis draws on Foucault's concept of governmentality, whereby control is exercised at a distance, through the manipulation of apparent freedom within a context of actual regulation and control.

This chapter is written at a time when standards and standardised tests have been introduced by almost all the states in the USA, ostensibly as a means of increasing student learning. In addition to these developments at state level, new Federal legislation requires that states test all students in reading and mathematics yearly in grades three through eight and at least once in grades ten through twelve, with additional subject area tests to be implemented at a later date. While research indicates that such efforts may not result in students learning more, politicians and representatives at the federal and state levels, including state departments of education, continue to promote the concepts of standards and testing as essential to improving education. In New York, the State Education Department (SED) has created standards for all the subject areas and has instituted standardised tests in a variety of subject areas and grade levels. Elementary students are required to take standardised tests in grades four, five, six, and eight.[1] High school students take standardised Regents exams in five subject areas.[2] These are high-stakes exams: they are used to compare teachers, students, schools, and school districts; and passing the exams has become a graduation requirement for students leaving High School.

The rise of testing and the decline of learning

The implementation of high-stakes standardised tests in New York has resulted in an increased drop-out rate, especially for students of colour, students for whom English is a second language, students living in poverty, and students with disabilities (Monk, Sipple and Killeen 2001). Elementary teachers report that they are pressured to spend more time preparing students for the tests given at their own or subsequent grade levels and less time teaching those subject areas not tested. For example, fourth grade teachers are pressured to prepare students not only to do well on the English Language Arts exam, the first standardised exam given to elementary students, but also to prepare fourth graders for the social studies exam given in the fall of fifth grade. The pressure placed on fourth grade teachers is causing many of them to request transfers to other grades or to resign from teaching. (Goodnough 2001; Monk, Sipple and Killeen 2002). Secondary teachers report that they devote increased time to teaching toward the test.

Furthermore, the Regents graduation requirement undermines the innovative programs of the twenty-eight primarily urban[3] high schools that comprise the New York Performance Standards Consortium (hereafter the Consortium Schools). In lieu of the Regents exams and the curriculum that prepares students for the exams, these schools have used an integrated theme-based curriculum and performance-based assessments[4] to achieve student success rates significantly greater than comparable schools in their neighborhood (New York Performance Standards Consortium 2001). The SED requirement that Consortium School students must now pass the exams in order to graduate necessitates that Consortium School teachers devote substantial time to covering the material in the five tested subject areas, thus undermining the interdisciplinary curriculum.

In the hope of retaining their successful approach, the Consortium Schools appealed to SED to continue their exemption from the Regents exams. The appeal was unsuccessful, and the Coalition Schools subsequently brought a lawsuit against SED.[5] To date, they have lost at the two lower court levels. Because the prospects of winning at the last and highest court appear bleak, the Consortium Schools have turned their attention to overturning the regulations through legislative remedies. While this route initially appeared unpromising, over the last year the media have revealed how the Board of Regents has manipulated test scores and altered literacy passages on exams without the authors' permission (Bracey 2002), prompting the legislature to call for hearings regarding the Regents exams.

Perhaps even more more significant is that New York has implemented a system of testing and accountability that obscures the State's[6] intervention into school districts which, historically, have been locally controlled. Because it is generally unacceptable, particularly for political conservatives, to advocate direct governmental intervention into social institutions, the politicians have derived a system through which educators can be controlled from a distance. It is to the means by which this control is exercised that I now turn my attention.

Governmentality and the discourse of neo-liberal economics, fairness, and objectivity

I analyse statements by SED officials and other policy-makers to argue that the testing and accountability movement reflects a major shift in who controls education and for what purposes, showing how the persuasive rhetoric of specific discourses is used to redefine the purpose of education and the problem of educational inequality. My analysis draws on Foucault's notion of governmentality, which shifts the analysis away from 'what happened and why?' to 'asking what authorities of various sorts wanted to happen, in relation to problems defined how, in pursuit of what objectives, through what strategies and techniques?' (Rose 1999: 20) Foucault's work analyses how social institutions, ranging from mental hospitals and prisons to schools, exercised power and disciplinary processes that work to support 'morally and intellectually validated schemes of social improvement, therapy and order, which operate by identifying and correcting various forms of individual deviation from a norm' (Gordon 2001: xvii). For Foucault, government necessarily has to do with the disciplining and normalising of populations, and governmentality is '[t]he ensemble formed by the institutions, procedures, analysis, and reflections, the calculations and tactics that allow the exercise of this very specific albeit complex form of power' (Foucault (edited collection) 2001: 219–220). It is these 'institutions, procedures, analysis, reflections, calculations and tactics' that are the focus of this chapter. I explore how the processes of governmentality in New York have brought about significant changes in how we understand social and economic aims, the meaning of freedom, and the relation between the individual and the state. At the level of the educational system, these changes constitute transformations in the purposes of schooling, the definition of knowledge, and the technologies of testing and accountability that render students' learning calculable and amenable, and discipline and normalise the profession of teaching.

To bring about these changes, the State policy-makers in New York have combined three principle discourses – the discourses of economic productivity, fairness and objectivity – using them to justify intervention into the lives of teachers and students and to exercise control at a distance through the tactics of testing, auditing and accountability. I describe each of these discourses briefly then analyse the way in which they link to policy, both globally and locally.

The primary discourse is that of neo-liberal economic theory. While education policy-makers do not usually provide an explicit economic theory behind their proposals, they do frequently cite the need to respond to global economic competition. For neo-liberals, economic competitiveness requires that we hold schools and teachers accountable for educating students to become productive workers. Further, neo-liberals desire to increase education's efficiency so that educational costs and, therefore governmental expenditures, can be minimised. Economic growth and corporate profits, rather than other criteria such as quality of life, become the dominant lens through which policy decisions are made.

Second, SED officials cite fairness as a rationale for revising school structures and practices. They argue that because most schools typically had two tracks (or streams), one resulting in the generally more rigorous Regents (NY State) diploma and the other in the non-Regents (local) diploma, those students who enrolled in the non-Regents courses, typically students of colour and living in poverty, received an inferior education.

Lastly, the professed need for objectivity provides a third rationale for standardised tests. Officials argue that because teachers evaluate students subjectively, standardised tests are necessary at the elementary and secondary levels. Standardised tests ostensibly eliminate the possibility that students will be graded unfairly.

These discourses and practices have resulted in a testing and accountability system that centralises the setting of educational and curricular goals at the State level and diminishes input by teachers, parents, and students at the local level (Rose 1999: 49). Moreover, auditing teachers through a testing and accountability system explicitly questions teachers' competency and undermines the trust placed in teachers as professionals (Rose 1999: 155).

The discourse of neo-liberalism

Neo-liberal economic theory rose, writes Parenti (1999), as a corporate and political response to the hard fought struggles by workers, students, and the poor for an extension of personal and labour rights beginning after World War II. Until the election of President Reagan, African Americans and people of colour had some success fighting for the right to vote, equal education, and welfare rights. Women fought for equal rights in the workplace and home. Post-secondary students fought for free speech and the right to be treated as adults. Workers fought for workplace protection and higher wages.

In response, corporations and governments in the US and other industrialised countries developed policies aimed at reducing personal rights and the power of workers, and promoting economic growth and corporate profits. Neo-liberal economic policies emphasise, as Rose writes, the restructuring of the social:

> Social government must be restructured in the name of an economic logic, and economic government must create and sustain the central elements of economic well-being such as the enterprise form and competition. As this advanced liberal diagram develops, the relation of the social and economic is rethought. All aspects of social behavior are now reconceptualised along economic lines – as calculative actions undertaken through the universal human faculty of choice. Choice is seen as dependent upon a relative assessment of costs and benefits of 'investment' in the light of environmental contingencies. All manner of social undertakings – health, welfare, education, insurance – can be reconstrued in terms of their contribution to the development of human capital.
>
> (Rose 1999: 141–2)

The adoption of neo-liberal economic theory represents a significant shift in relation to the state's role in promoting social welfare. Under the Keynesian economic theory which preceded neo-liberalism, governments intervened in the social sphere by funding social services (education, health, welfare, etc.) as public goods and ensuring consumer demand through deficit spending and unemployment insurance (Robertson 2000: 95). In contrast, neo-liberal economic theory emphasises reducing tax and regulatory burdens on corporations and decreasing or privatising social services, so that individuals and corporations can devote funds to economic expansion. By promoting economic growth over other goals, neo-liberal educational discourses emphasise holding schools accountable for efficiently producing workers who contribute to economic expansion.

For those who adopt a neo-liberal approach, then, education needs to be restructured as a competitive enterprise preparing students to be productive workers. Such policies are being adopted throughout the world. Australian educational analyst Blackmore observes that 'Education has, in most instances, been reshaped to become the arm of national economic policy, defined both as the problem (in failing to provide a multi-skilled flexible workforce) and the solution (by upgrading skills and creating a source of national export earnings)' (2000: 134). Blackmore summarises the consequences of these discourses for educational policy as having 'shifted from input and process to outcomes, from the liberal to the vocational, from education's intrinsic value to its instrumental value, and from qualitative to quantitative measures of success' (2000: 134). Over the last decade, the discourse of neo-liberalism has become so prevalent that few question whether there are any alternatives.

Proponents of standards, testing, and accountability insist that such reforms are necessary for the nation's economic success. Louis Gerstner, Jr., past CEO of IBM and Chair of the two National Summits on Education, recently responded to criticism of standardised testing in New York by writing: 'Any retreat from our national and state efforts now not only would harm students but would limit our competitive position in the global marketplace' (2002: A31). This explicit link between schooling and economic productivity is summed up in a statement from the US National Alliance of Business (NAB):

> A standards-driven reform agenda should include content and performance standards, alignment of school processes with the standards, assessments that measure student achievement against world-class levels of excellence, information about student and school performance, and accountability for results'
>
> (Smith/NAB nd: 4).[7]

Such restructuring has been accepted as the inevitable outcome of our modern, global society and provides a powerful rationale for the increasing control over education. Pronouncements such as that by an

Undersecretary of Education under the Clinton administration, that schools must meet the 'ever changing challenges of international competition and the workplace' (Smith and Scoll 1995: 390), are so ubiquitous that they escape scrutiny.

The assumption that neo-liberal economics must guide our thinking has become so dominant that the voices of those calling for alternative social conceptions emphasising the quality of life measured not in material goods but in terms of the environment, culture, health, and welfare are largely silenced. Consequently, many have acquiesced to the notion that we live in a globalised society in which neo-liberal economic policies are inevitable. As Bourdieu states: 'A whole set of presuppositions is being imposed as self-evident: it is taken for granted that maximum growth, and therefore productivity and competitiveness, are the ultimate and sole goal of human actions; or that economic forces cannot be resisted' (1998: 31).

However, given the long-time conservative rhetoric abhorring state intervention into people's lives, we need to ask how we can explain the rise of a system in which local democratic control2 of schools is undermined by the state. In answering that question, we need to analyze the discourses supporting standardised testing over other means of assessment and the organisational forms and technologies that make such systems both possible and acceptable.

The discourse of fairness

The acceptance of standards, standardised testing and accountability did not occur solely because those in power and the mainstream media have promoted it. Those promoting the discourse of standards and testing have been obliged to develop rationales that fit into larger truth claims about education in society. In particular, for the past two decades, both neo-liberals and conservatives have criticised schools for failing to educate students adequately (Apple 2001), and it is to this criticism that the discourse of fairness appeals. While it is true that the economic disparity between urban and suburban schools and the tracking of students of colour and students from working-class families towards low-status qualifications has led to unequal outcomes in the US, current neo-liberal policy constitutes a form of control by which, as Rose states, 'government continually seeks to give itself a form of truth – establish a kind of ethical basis for its action' (1999: 27).

The proponents of testing and accountability justify their proposals, in part, on the moral argument of fairness. New York State's educational policy-makers, including the past Chancellor and present Commissioner of Education, justify the changes on the grounds that standards and standardised testing are the only way to ensure that all students, including students of colour and those living in poverty, have an opportunity to learn. They argue that it is these same students who, because of the end of industrialism and the rise of globalisation, can no longer be permitted to fail. All students must succeed educationally to ensure that the individual and the nation succeeds economically.

Proponents of standards, testing and accountability point out that, historically, our educational system has better served those students who are already advantaged. The Regents exam originated in New York in the mid-1800s as both a college entrance exam and as one means of standardising the curriculum (New York State Education Department 2002). However, over the last century the New York educational system has evolved into a two-track system, with Regents exams and curricula for college bound students and non-Regents courses for non-college bound students, with the latter courses dominated by working-class students and students of colour.

In order ostensibly to reduce the disparity, the SED eliminated the non-Regents or local diplomas, as described in the opening section of this chapter. Carl Hayden, the New York Chancellor of Education for the past six years, draws on the discourse of fairness to justify this development:

> The requirement that every child be brought to a Regents level of performance is revolutionary. It is a powerful lever for education equity. It is changing for the better the life prospects of millions of young people, particularly poor and minority children who in the past would have been relegated to a low standards path. Too often, these children emerged from school without the skills and knowledge needed for success in an increasingly complex economy.
>
> (Hayden 2001: 1, original emphasis)

However, the State's new requirement has only resulted in the increasing regulation of schools, curriculum, teaching, and students, while neither eliminating the two track system nor the disparity in educational opportunities between upper- and working-class students. The two-tier system persists, as more advantaged students who had previously enrolled in Regents courses are now strongly encouraged to enroll in honors, Advanced Placement, and International Baccalaureate courses, leaving the less advantaged students in the Regents track. Because the Regents plan has already increased the drop-out rate, particularly for English as Second Language Learners and students with special needs, the Regents have made the compulsory exams easier. The SED's claims that standardised testing improves the assessment process are weakened by the way in which the scoring of tests is manipulated: for example, for the most recent living environments exam, taken by most students, students only needed to answer 39 percent of the questions correctly; a result which the Board of Regents converted to a passing grade of 65 percent. Conversely, the exams for the advanced, non-required courses such as physics and chemistry have been made more difficult, to make the testing process appear more rigorous.

Furthermore, both qualitative and quantitative data regarding students' experiences raise doubts over whether politicians and educational bureaucrats really desire an improved and more equitable educational system. In New York, the gap in performance between the advantaged white middle-class students and disadvantaged working-class students and students of colour has increased, as has the drop-out rate for students in the poorer urban schools, while students for whom English is a second language left school at a 12% higher rate this year than last (Monk, Sipple, and Killeen 2001).

We can also ask what the State is doing to reduce the inequalities between school districts. Currently, New York's schools are the most segregated and the second most unequally funded in the United States. Because of the current economic slow down, the State's urban schools have received significant reductions in revenue. In the 2001–2002 school year the New York City public schools received one billion dollars less than the previous year (Kozol June 10, 2002). In January 2001, in response to a lawsuit from the Campaign for Fiscal Equity, a judge declared that New York's education finance system denied millions of New York City public school students their constitutional right to a sound basic education (Campaign for Fiscal Equity V. State of New York). However, Governor Pataki succeeded in having the decision reversed with the judges deciding that a 'sound basic education' consists of no more than an eighth grade education and that inadequate funding for new library stock is acceptable because there is nothing wrong with learning from the 'classics'.

Lastly, the requirement that all students must pass the five Regents exams effectively eliminates the Consortium Schools' programme as an alternative to traditional approaches to teaching. While the Consortium Schools have succeeded at graduating and sending to college a higher percentage of their students than comparable district high schools, the State has undermined their innovative practices.

There is one remaining discourse upon which policy-makers draw to justify these policies and practices: the discourse of objectivity.

The discourse of objectivity

The proponents of standards and testing situate their proposals within a particular epistemological context, arguing that the standards have been objectively determined and that standardised tests provide a valid and reliable means of assessing student learning. Such objective methods are required, they state, because teachers and administrators cannot be trusted to assess student learning objectively and accurately. Teacher generated assessment protocols and instruments are dismissed, within this discourse, as subjective and unreliable, and the fact that the tests assess only a small percentage of the State's standards and have questionable validity is effectively ignored. The implication that to adopt other meanings of assessment results automatically in a lowering of standards is embedded in this discourse of objectivity, as can be seen in Chancellor Hayden's response to the possibility of retaining performance assessment:

> there is an even greater danger. The least rigorous, the least valid, the least reliable approved alternative [assessment] is then available to any school. Which schools will be first in the race to the lowest common denominator? Those having the most trouble bringing all children to a Regents level of performance. Those keen to reacquire the low standard option lost when the RCT [Regents Competency Test] and the local diploma were abolished. Those that never

believed that all children can reach high standards. Were this to occur, it is all too apparent that poor and minority children would disproportionately bear the burden of diminished expectations.

(Hayden 2001: 2)

In an earlier memo Chancellor Hayden responded to school super-intendents who questioned the state testing regime by stating:

good districts anticipated the changes and put in strategies [to meet] standards. It is the ones who didn't anticipate who weren't paying attention who find themselves scrambling now [sic]. These hearings have provided a platform for some superintendents who never believed in higher standards to begin with and who never thought they'd have to implement them.

(Hayden 1999)

Similarly, Louis Gerstner, in responding to schools that protested against the New York statewide reading test, stated: 'But it's also the nature of some people to resist change, especially when compliance with a new policy involves real effort' (March 13, 2002: A31). Ironic-ally, these statements by Hayden and Gerstner ignore the fact that some of the schools most vocal in opposition have been from the most successful – in terms of test scores – suburban school districts

Finally, the discourse of objectivity draws on the image of testing as a system of accounting and auditing as a claim to validity. Thus stan-dardised testing appears objective even though the SED has provided no evidence of the tests' validity, nor whether the tests assess the State's standards, nor whether the grading practices are reasonable. This hold persists, writes Rose, because numbers appear to be an accurate reflection of what students learn. 'Numbers . . . actually con-stitute the domains they appear to represent, they render them repre-sentable in a docile form – a form amenable to the application of calculation and deliberation' (1999: 198). By this means, students' achievements are rendered docile, disciplined, and normalised.

Power and resistance: regaining control

As Barry, Osborne and Rose write, the intervention of the state into the life of the individual uses strategies that 'tie techniques of conduct into specific relations with the concerns of government' and 'reconnect, in a productive way, studies of the exercise of power at the 'molecular levels [in schools] with strategies to program power at a molar level' (1996: 13):

> public authorities seek to employ forms of expertise in order to govern society at a distance, without recourse to any direct forms of repression and intervention . . . Neo-liberalism, in these terms, involves less a retreat from governmental 'intervention' than a re-inscription of the techniques and expertise required for the exercise of government.
>
> (Barry *et al* 1996: 14)

Governmental and quasi-governmental organisations seek to govern without specifying exactly what must be done, instead presenting the requirements or standards as rational and non-controversial, and providing limitations on the ways in which they must be implemented. This gives teachers a false sense of choice and freedom. Political institutions 'conceive of these actors as subjects of responsibility, autonomy, and choice, and seek to act upon them through shaping and utilising their freedom' (Rose 1996a: 53–54). In response, we can use our freedom to push for a renewed focus on the process rather than the outcome of education; for liberal over vocational education; for a recognition of education's intrinsic rather than vocational value; and for qualitative rather than quantitative measures of success. Through the critique of the dominant discourses of economic productivity, fairness, and objectivity and their accompanying institutional practices, we can work towards regaining professionalism and control.

Acknowledgements

I would especially like to thank Camille Martina for her assistance in conceptualising and writing the chapter, and the students in my doctoral course, 'Issues in Teaching and Curriculum,' for their comments and questions.

Notes

1. Standardised tests are given in the fourth grade for English Language Arts, science, and math, fifth grade for social studies, and eighth grade for English Language Arts, science, social studies and math.
2. The five exams are English in grade 11; mathematics in grade 10; social studies (global studies in grade 10 and United States history in grade 11; and any one of earth science,

living environments, physics, or chemistry. Regents exams are also given for math in grade 11.

3. In the USA, 'urban' implies schools whose students are primarily students of colour and from low-income families.

4. The Consortium Schools have developed a system of assessment that requires students to use multiple means of exhibiting learning, including presentations, performances, writing, and oral exams.

5. For more information on the Consortium Schools and their dispute with the New York State Education Department see the paper co-authored with Camille Martina, 'Resisting the Tyranny of Tests: The Battle for New York,' presented at the first Discourse, Power, Resistance Conference, University of Plymouth, UK, April 2002.

6. Hereafter 'State' refers to New York State in particular and 'state' refers to local, state and national governments in general.

7. The National Alliance of Business 2002 Conference (November 5–8) focused on 'The New Era of Education Reform: Corporate Opportunities to Strengthen Tomorrow's Workforce.' Topics included: 'The Business Role in PreK-16 Learning: Aligning the Knowledge Supply Chain' and 'Aligning Expectations: The Role of Tests in Translating High School Student Competencies to Higher Education and the Workplace.' See <http://www.conference-board.org/conference/conference>

5

Power and Resistance in Further Education: The discursive work of negotiating identities

ROGER HARRISON, JULIA CLARKE, RICHARD
EDWARDS and FIONA REEVE

Roger Harrison and his colleagues argue that the discursive construction of flexibility, as a feature of further education, has produced a range of responses from academic staff. Rather than learning to understand themselves as eagerly responsive to the changing demands of the flexible organisation, academics position themselves strategically, in the interests of survival, but also with the best interests of students stubbornly in mind. This chapter brings the practitioner to the centre of the debate about power and resistance: we see what lecturers and teachers actually do in response to discursive pressure, preparing us for the further interrogation of practice in Quinn's and Colley's chapters.

Introduction

This chapter draws on a two year empirical research project (1999–2001). Our intention was to examine the work which discourses of flexibility perform in constructing certain understandings of what it means to work and learn in further education in the UK (Edwards *et al* 2001). We have drawn on three interviews, giving voice to only a small selection of our informants. The selection has been made in order to illuminate discussion of the ways in which lecturers' identities are shaped and reshaped in the context of further education colleges.

The concept of flexibility has developed largely from an analysis of, and a prescription for, changes in the economy and workplace. Flexibility emerged as a response to the economic problems of inflation and lack of growth in the 1970s and blossomed in the context of the free market economics of the 1980s and 1990s, infiltrating the public and voluntary as well as the private sector. Discourses of flexibility suggest both different ways of working – a shift away from job demarcation in the cause of efficiency and effectiveness – and a different disposition towards working – one in which workers are enterprising and self reliant in responding to the needs of 'customers' and learners. Here we focus on dispositions: the ways in which lecturing staff in further education talk about themselves and their work roles; how they construct and make sense of their own professional identities. The analysis follows others (Avis 1999; Farrell 2000) in viewing the workplace as a site of struggle in which identity or subject positions are discursively constructed. However, this is not to suggest that new identities associated with discourses of the flexible worker are unproblematically taken up. Here we are using the notion of work put forward by Farrell (2000) who argues that employees do not simply take or reject the discourses of management in the workplace, but also work them, that is, create meanings other than those which might have been intended. We explore the ways in which the language of flexibility becomes a resource that is worked to construct and reconstruct a variety of identity positions.

Discourse and power in Further Education

In the context of further education in the UK discourses of flexibility are powerful in two senses. First, colleges are increasingly being required to conduct themselves according to the management and employment practices of the flexible firm and the learning organisation. Since incorporation following the 1992 Further and Higher Education Act colleges have been 'launched on a tide of market forces' (Capizzi, Carter and Davies 1998) which has affected all aspects of college life from employment practices to organisational culture (Spours and Lucas 1996). Here flexibility stands for more business-like ways of working, including rationalisation of provision, enhanced institutional responsiveness to the market and short-term contracts of employment. Second, in their role as providers of learning opportunities colleges are required to provide more flexible forms of learning to service the requirements of the economy and the demands of lifelong learning. Here flexibility stands for improving access through curriculum innovation, with a particular emphasis on new technologies, modular courses, work-based learning, credit accumulation and transfer.

Further Education plays a pivotal role in the UK government's overall strategy of promoting a flexible or learning society, operating at the interface between education, training and employment. It is therefore especially in further education that traditional institutional and pedagogical boundaries are being challenged. The scope and speed of change in further education has placed considerable pressure on teaching staff to adapt to, and make sense of, shifting policy agendas which position competitiveness, efficiency and accountability alongside commitments to the goals of widening access and countering social and economic disadvantage. Reporting from one study, Capizzi, Carter and Davies (1998) comment on the resulting challenges to teaching staff as they seek to make sense of their own roles in a context where different agendas are frequently in play:

> In this context, teaching staff have had to manage not only their workload but also construct some explanation of what is going on and where they fit in the 'new FE' . . . The situation is one of prevailing ambiguity and change which has implications for staff not only in terms of what they can and must do, but also in terms of their own identity. (41)

In another study of the position of lecturers in further education James Avis also suggests that changes in teaching and learning practices have resulted in an 'on-going transformation of what it is to be a college lecturer' (Avis 1999: 260). Along with other commentators (Ainley and Bailey 1997, Yarrow and Esland 1999), Avis associates these changes with the political dominance of the new right, the shift towards economistic and managerial priorities in the workplace, and the consequent need to remake the mould of the public sector professional. For Avis the workplace is seen as a site of struggle in which the values of liberal humanism are threatened by a subtle and persuasive manifestation of reformist capitalism. While Avis' analysis is in some ways useful, it achieves only a partial fit with our own research data, which suggests that the boundaries within the site of struggle are more permeable and shifting than those which he describes. We would also take issue with the dualistic opposition which is set up by associating economistic and managerial priorities with the new right, and liberal humanist priorities with the political left, since each of these positions have themselves been re-worked and re-presented by New Labour since it came to government in 1997. This suggests the site of struggle itself as a more complex and mobile target than Avis' analysis allows.

Avis' interpretation suggests the operation of power as hierarchical and top-down, something which is held and wielded over others by institutions and individuals in authority. It is closely associated with a discourse of standards and accountability emanating from government and college managers in a calculated attempt to discipline and control the activities of college lecturers. In presenting his analysis Avis (2000: 48) explicitly draws on Foucault's earlier writings which appear to suggest a rather monolithic view of discourse as a regime of truth, an operation of power which acts to limit the possibilities for individual freedom. Reviewing the analysis of the workings of power in *Discipline and Punish* 1991a Gordon notes that 'Foucault's representation of society as a network of subjugating power seemed to preclude the possibility of meaningful individual freedom' (Gordon 1991: 4). Whilst this analysis has some resonance with our own data, it fails to capture the complexity, ambiguity and mobility of lecturers' positionings in relation to discourses of flexibility both within the college and in the world beyond.

Here interpretations which offer a more fruitful approach to analysis move away from an emphasis on discourse as constituting symbolic systems and social orders towards ones which draw attention to the mutually constituting relationship between discourses and the social systems in which they function. We therefore draw on Foucault's later work, his 'genealogical' writings, which suggests a more active and productive dimension of power. Howarth (2000) describes a process of development in Foucault's writing in which he moves from an understanding of discourse as constituting everything – meanings, objects, social relationships, subjectivities – to a more strategic perspective in which discourses are the means for different forces to advance their interests and projects, whilst also providing points of resistance for counter strategies to develop (Howarth 2000: 49).

From this standpoint 'power in a society is never a fixed or closed regime, but rather an endless and open strategic game' (Gordon 1991: 5). Discourse is neither stable nor monolithic but constantly in play and always containing the seeds of its own contradictions and oppositions. As Foucault (1979) writes in *The History of Sexuality*:

> . . . discourse can be both an instrument and an effect of power, but also a hindrance, a stumbling block, a point of resistance and a starting point for an opposing strategy. Discourse transmits and produces power; it reinforces it, but also undermines and exposes it, renders it fragile and makes it possible to thwart it. (100–1)

In Foucault's terms disciplinary power is not simply repressive, as it acts to develop capacities, inclinations and dispositions which are seen as more appropriate and productive. Thus, though people are subject to exercises of power, they are nonetheless subjects, that is, capable of judgement and action. Here therefore disciplinary power works not through repression but through the development of individuals' 'dispositions and habits' (Ransom 1997: 156). This is a 'pastoral' form of governance which 'enables individuals to actively participate in disciplinary regimes through investing their own identity, subjectivities and desires with those ascribed to them by certain knowledgeable discourses' (Usher and Edwards 1998: 215). It is this active engagement in discursive practices which opens up spaces and opportunities for individuals to adopt their own strategies and negotiate their own positionings.

Identity is taken here not as an essential category, the coherent, unified subject of the Enlightenment, but as historically and culturally produced. The stories through which people construct their identities are not transparent insights into their essential selves but 'continuously revised, biographical narratives' (Giddens 1991: 5) which incorporate a variety of existing cultural texts which are woven together to 'make-up' identity (Hacking 1986: 234). What Hall refers to as 'identification' is understood as 'a construction, a process never completed' (Hall 1996: 2), in which identity can never be singular or unified but always fragmented, fractured and 'in process'. In studying those who work and learn in the context of further education colleges, theoretical perspectives that view identity as discursively constructed, and identification as ongoing work, provide an interpretative stance from which to view the accounts of learners and workers throughout the institutions.

Here we look at three case studies of members of staff drawn from both of the colleges involved in the research project, focusing on their dispositions to work and the ways in which they construct boundaries around their professional identities. These three individuals have been chosen not because they are representative but because they represent particular discursive strategies through which workers in further education construct their identity positions.

Discursive positioning

Deborah is a full time lecturer on a temporary contract. Here she describes her reading of social and institutional expectations of the work role:

> . . . it seems that people don't want, or society doesn't allow, them to be pigeon holed. You have to be able to skim and skate from one area to another. And I think that is good in some ways because you can, in theory, cover everybody's job, but the problem is . . . we excel in different aspects at different types of work so I don't see how that works actually in reality.

Deborah deploys two telling metaphors to describe the sort of identity and working practices required of teaching staff in further education. First, a refusal of the 'pigeonhole', with all that this image represents in terms of fixity, stability, inflexibility. The more desirable form of identity is flexible and adaptable, better suited to the 'skimming and skating' which is a necessary part of the job. The metaphor of the pigeonhole is significant in relation to discourses of autonomy and choice, which are closely associated with those of flexibility. The qualities or characteristics that are seen as desirable within these discourses are those of self-reliance, personal responsibility and enterprise (du Gay 1996). Though apparently offering the opportunities of choice, the discourse of the flexible and autonomous worker does not necessarily empower, since, as Farrell (2000) observes, employees are already schooled into particular forms of subjectivity which tend to align their own goals with those of the organisation. So as Deborah suggests, her ways of working are more the result of necessity than choice, since 'you *have to* be able to skim and skate' (our emphasis).

The effects of this are seen as ambiguous and contradictory, as acknowledged gains in work role flexibility are countered by a lack of expertise in some areas. Teaching staff are never able to settle in one work role or give their undivided attention to one task as they constantly strive to cover a wide remit. Whilst explicitly acknowledging role flexibility as 'good in some ways' Deborah proceeds to undermine it by pointing to the losses in efficiency resulting from flexible working practices, culminating in her assessment that 'I don't see how that works actually'. In doing so she draws attention to the value of role specialisation and job demarcation, part of an older discourse of professional expertise, criticised by some as lacking relevance to the post-Fordist workplace.

Deborah positions herself as an apprentice in her work role and something of an outsider to the college. She is relatively new to further education, seeing her move into this area of employment as 'practical' and 'mercenary'. Her current post is a one year contract to cover maternity leave. She sees this as a way of checking out teaching in further education as a possible career move – 'so I am here to experience how it is and to see whether I want to be doing this later on'. She adopts the tone of an ironic outsider, using humour to distance herself from the jargon of the college – 'when I first came here the students' timetables were in a form of Swahili' – and from the rhetoric of flexibility. Deborah is able to take a sceptical position towards the discourses of the college, maintaining her own sense of control and autonomy in a context where her employment remains tenuous.

Whilst prepared to acknowledge that flexible ways of working can be 'good in some ways' Deborah also points to the ways in which they can have a negative effect on students:

> The students get pushed to the end sometimes because the system's so flexible and so reactive the very purpose for our being sometimes gets forgotten or lost under paperwork . . . and because of one crisis following another, people are running down the corridor going to a lesson, then the room gets moved or there isn't the right resource for teaching, so in terms of disorder . . . to me it's important that students have continuity and that they are valued and that they are here to learn, and I don't quite understand how they are going to feel organised and respected . . .

She positions herself as on the side of students and learning. Flexibilities in the college's organisational systems and in the delivery of teaching and learning are presented as undermining the needs of learners for continuity, order and respect. We might recognise the identity of the teacher represented in Avis' (1998) analysis of the post-Fordist workplace, attempting to be self regulating and empowered in a context where the rules of engagement are defined by others to serve the interests of others. What is also present is a discursive move that aligns the speaker with the 'learner-centred' aspiration that lies at the heart of discourses of flexibility. Whilst positioning herself as critical towards aspects of college practices, Deborah simultaneously and strategically places herself on the side of learners. It is, after all, the achievement of greater relevance to learner or customer needs which provides the rationale for flexibilities in the institution and the curriculum. But Deborah might also be invoking an older liberal humanist discourse that still underpins the practices of much post-compulsory education. Writers from John Dewey to Stephen Brookfield have argued for a learner-centred curriculum that takes as its starting point the lived experience of the learner. How far this learner-centred discourse is compatible with a customer-centred and market-driven discourse of the flexible college is a question raised but not answered by Deborah's observations.

Identification with the interests of students is a position taken up with passion and commitment by Ren, a full time lecturer and a trade union representative. He nails his colours to the mast in no uncertain terms: 'I love the students but hate the organisation.' Ren is comfortable using the language of flexibility, consistently interpreting it as part of a systematic managerial discourse designed to govern the conduct of staff. The corporate discourse of flexibility has certainly come to colonise his everyday life, but not perhaps in ways the institution might have anticipated or wished. His analysis is grounded in his experience of the further education context but forms part of an ideology that goes beyond this, presenting a more general analysis of the condition of society. 'For people in most jobs . . . it seems that flexibility is now the thing and insecurity is also sort of snapping at your heels so people are much more pressured.'

In the context of the college flexibility is represented as acting in the interests of management, not teaching staff:

> There is some very marginal flexibility but it's mostly dictated by management needs rather than my own needs . . . what the Principal wants in terms of flexibility is an open contract, you know, they say right you've got 38 weeks, we want you to come in any old time. We don't want you to make a distinction between contact time and non-contact time and you know as a human being and a teacher as well as a Union official there's no way I'm going to swallow that kind of flexibility.

Resistance to 'that kind of flexibility' is supported by reference to an identity beyond his role as a teacher – and to certain norms and standards which are associated with being a 'human being' and which are also backed up by the activities of the Union. For Ren his sense of identity derives from his loyalties to subject teaching and to his students. Standing against flexibility is represented as standing on the side of students against managerial practices that seek to distort and disrupt the liberating potential of learning. Ren's analysis echoes that of Avis (1998) who describes modernising changes in the curriculum as a 'move' which 'breaks the link between scholarship and learning' (75) and is marked by a displacement of the 'subject specialist' by the 'learning facilitator' as the more desirable form of professional identity. Teaching staff in both colleges were engaged in negotiating this shift in values and practices in the knowledge that how they managed the transition would have a direct impact on their career progression. Locating his own affiliations with subject teaching might rule Ren out from career advancement, but it does have compensations. One of these is allowing him to indulge in a discourse of derision, ridiculing the behaviour of managers:

> . . . we get a lot of panic here among managers who have situations they can't deal with, classes they can't cover and they want to be able to tell someone to go in and just, you know, 'I don't care what you do, be there'.

In this extract Ren echoes Deborah's description of 'one crisis following another', but the meanings each constructs from the phenomenon of crisis management, and the identity positions adopted in response to it, are quite distinct. Here we see the complex and contextualized nature of meaning-making as each draws on their own histories, circumstances and situated understandings to produce subtly different accounts.

For Ren, flexibility is associated with a managerial approach that is obsessed with standards and the measurement of performance:

> I think it's like the five year plan in the Soviet Union. The only way people could survive was by people faking it. So I think any chance I get personally to fake my paperwork to make my results look good I will use . . .

In Ren's analysis discourses of flexibility are linked with the operations of power, experienced as a top-down imposition from one ideologically coherent group (managers) to another (teachers). His position is strongly ideological, allowing no concessions towards a discourse he interprets as similarly ideologically driven, located in Thatcherite notions of an enterprise culture. Perhaps unsurprisingly he does not see a future for himself in further education management.

Sally is a full time lecturer. She began her own career as a mature learner in the same further education college where she now works:

> So I came here and here were these 16 to 17 year olds . . . doing part time GCSEs alongside me who was 35 and I just thought this is where I want to work, this is what I want to do when I get trained, so I kind of fought really hard to get a teaching practice here and to kind of wheedle my way in through part time work . . .

Sally identifies teaching as the area of her work which gives her the most satisfaction and reports spending a good deal of time sorting out the problems of students in her group. She is critical of managers whose only interest is in performance indicators rather than individual students:

> . . . somebody on the top floor above us here looks at the numbers – and they do – because they bump into you in the corridor and say 'oh your numbers are down (Sally) and you just want to tell them about the histories of these individual kids, but they don't want to hear stories they want numbers . . . we're always told 'we're not interested in anecdotes about why this wonderful student got pregnant or went back to Somalia or whatever', you know, 'did you retain them or didn't you?'

Sally invokes the histories of individual students, juxtaposing a discourse of personalised and contextualised life experiences with a depersonalised managerial discourse of effectiveness and efficiency, where anecdotes are judged to be a less reliable measure of student performance than retention figures. The way in which Sally distances herself from this latter position suggests an empathy with the individual circumstances and life stories of those she teaches which is neither recognised nor rewarded within the administrative structures and processes of the college.

However, she also finds herself drawn towards activities beyond the immediate teaching role:

> . . . some people are more like me, like still have a lot of energy and get asked to do things and keep themselves sort of visible, if you know what I mean. Like . . . you'll be the one that offers to do it, who wants to go on the curriculum board, 'oh I'll do it', because I couldn't stand just putting my head down and teaching all the time and not, not being bothered about the wider college environment.

This is a 'can do' approach that fits well with images of the flexible organisation projected by popular management writers such as Peters and Waterman (1982); staffed by 'charged up people' who go out and become 'winners' for the organisation and themselves. However, Sally is also pragmatic and careful to put boundaries on her willingness to take on new roles. She has recently taken on the role of 'lead tutor' which she describes as 'a sort of semi-management responsibility' on the basis that it gives her remission from some class teaching but she draws the line at further involvement in management. She sees managers, such as her boss, as 'go-getters' who work all hours, and is protective of her own life outside the college:

> I said I don't want a management job, I don't want to lose my holidays and all that but I'm really happy to do it for the hours so I'm really not pushing this management job because my holidays and my life are very important to me . . .

A feature of much contemporary management literature is the move towards blurring the boundaries between employees' home and work lives, as 'corporate discourses come to colonise everyday lives' (Farrell 2000: 20). Whilst for some this provides a useful means of harnessing the full potential of the worker, for others it represents an attempt to reshape identity, incorporating the whole person (mind, body and soul) into the productive enterprise (du Gay 1996). Sally is cautiously embracing flexibility of role, but within strict limits and in return for tangible gains. She is able to exploit the spaces which flexibility creates by presenting herself as an entrepreneurial employee, but only to a certain extent and in certain contexts. She might be identified with those 'enterprising capacities' which du Gay (1996) suggests lead individuals 'to conduct themselves with boldness and vigour, to calculate for their own advantage, to drive themselves hard, and to accept risks in the pursuit of goals' (154). Yet this would considerably oversimplify her position. She is critical of management practices, particularly those associated with quality control, and could easily find herself in alliance with colleagues like Ren on issues of student support. If the success of the entrepreneurial, flexible organisation depends upon blurring the boundaries between the personal goals and objectives of employees and those of their employers it does not appear to have succeeded in this case. For Sally the boundary between her home and work lives appears to be secure, and any collusions she might enter into are carefully negotiated.

A multiplicity of discourses

These are selections from the interview data that have been chosen for the ways in which they represent the operation of discourse, power and resistance in shaping the identities of lecturers. The story being told through the three case studies is one of multiple and complex positioning within discourses which draw on and work contemporary notions of flexibility. What emerges is a complex image of lecturers in further education actively exploiting the fuzziness of their role boundaries, and the ambiguous spaces in the flexible workplace, as they construct and re-construct a variety of identity positions. Those offered here can be taken neither as definitive nor stable, but constantly in play and subject to change as the subjects of this study engage with the risky and uncertain enterprise of 'emigration to new niches of activity and identity' (Beck 1992: 194).

We have attempted through the analysis to indicate some of the ways in which our informants were both subject to the power of institutional discourses of flexibility and worker identity and also active in constructing their own discourses and identity positions. These speakers were constantly working – interpreting and adapting – their understandings of flexibility in relation to the circumstances and context of their work, and then again in the context of the research interview. Flexibility supplies some of the 'discursive hardware'

(Weber 2002) with which they were able to articulate an account of their identities which they felt appropriate for that particular time and place. In this sense neither flexibility nor identity positions are stable notions that can be researched, defined and understood, but instead are fluid and transitory, produced and interpreted to achieve specific effects at particular times and in particular places. What is suggested here is that the relationship between individuals and powerful discourses, such as that of flexibility, is neither deterministic nor reducible to positions of compliance or resistance. Rather, such discourses form part of the symbolic and material resources through which college lecturers are able to make and re-make complex, contingent, contextualized and multi-faceted constructions of what it means to work as a lecturer in further education.

This chapter is an edited version of an article in *Research in Post-Compulsory Education,* 2003, Volume 7 number 1.

6

The Ethnographic Self as Hired Hand: Reflecting on researching educational partnerships

JOCEY QUINN

Jocey Quinn's insistence on asking the awkward questions and refusing to accept the rhetoric of 'what works' takes her into the unexplored borderlands between ethical inquiry and contract research. Following Atkinson and Hursh, she challenges the assumptions behind political demands for accountability; and anticipating Gale's chapter, she argues for participative, discursive frameworks for learning. She undertakes a ruthless interrogation of the forces that shape participation in policy led initiatives: a theme which is taken up again in Colley's chapter on the myth of mentoring.

Introduction: from quest to task

In this chapter I bring together two very different facets of educational research: those of 'high' policy and 'deep' reflexivity. Although educational researchers have been admonished to reflect on the significance of their personal constitution within fieldwork as 'ethnographic selves' (Coffey 1999), in practice they are often engaged as 'hired hands' to conduct research projects which have short time frames and are purely outcome driven. Some attention has been paid to the particular issues faced by contract researchers, but there has been little reflection on the systematic dichotomy between the ideal of reflexivity and the exigencies of 'quick and dirty' research, and the consequences that follow. If reflexivity is a quintessential part of the research process, but policy is largely determined by unreflexive research, the implications are deeply serious. I analyse these implications through a situated study of a particular policy-led research project.

The chapter is contextualised by a personal and professional shift, which is certainly not universal amongst researchers, but still common enough to have some resonance. The shift was the move from full time PhD student, absorbed in the tormenting luxury of 'my own work', to full time Research Fellow available for hire by funding bodies. Much of my time as a PhD student had been engaged in interesting thoughts about my own positioning as a researcher and how this influenced my methodology and interpretations, inspired by ongoing debate in feminist research. The importance of reflexivity to my work was axiomatic: but was it also idealistic and unrealistic? This chapter examines one of the first large scale pieces of hired hand research I was involved in post PhD, in which my colleagues and I cheerfully abandoned any attempt at the cherished goal of reflexivity. I do not think this slippage from theory to practice is uncommon, and this chapter is argued in a spirit of curiosity, not self flagellation; my purpose here is to try to understand the implications of such major shifts for the research community as a whole.

The research I shall refer to, commissioned by the Higher Education Funding Council for England (HEFCE), explored the development of partnerships set up to widen participation in Higher Education (Thomas *et al* 2001). Set to a tight three-month deadline, it took up a major part of my life, assuming such importance that many things were sidelined in an attempt to complete it. So why is it that I can hardly remember what happened, what it felt like, what thoughts and feelings it inspired? Unlike my PhD, it was a task rather than a quest, and simply did not involve the same level of investment. Perhaps this is only a good thing: to live as a permanent PhD student would be a fresh hell indeed, but once the research was over, I pondered the dichotomy between the thesis and the research report. Could, and should, the two ever be reconciled? What happens to the ethnographic self when it is used as a hired hand, and what happens to research when the ethnographic self is pushed aside?

High policy: partnerships and the pantheon of 'what works'

Before moving to analyse our research on educational partnerships, it is necessary to understand the policy context into which this research falls. It has been well demonstrated, particularly by Atkinson (2000d, 2002a and in her chapter in this book), that in terms of educational policy the UK government holds very tightly to a 'utilitarian doctrine' (Goodson 1999: 286–7) of 'effectiveness' and 'what works'. Despite heated debates about the inviolability of 'evidence based practice' (see for example Hargreaves 1996, Hammersley 1997, Elliot 2001, Oakley 2001) there is little indication that a shift towards more reflexive policy is underway. Within this frame, the issue of widening participation, which ultimately has broad ranging epistemological and ethical dimensions, has been reduced to a numbers game. Reaching the government's target of 50% of 18–30 year olds benefiting from Higher Education (HE) by 2010 has been described as 'politically non-negotiable' (Newby 2002), and therefore constitutes an urgent task that has been couched in crudely measurable terms. In the context of this policy drive, partnerships hold a central position in the pantheon of 'what works'. Substantial and projected investment (both rhetorical and financial) is currently being made in partnerships, with HEFCE concluding that 'significant investment is needed to achieve the aim of increasing HE participation through stronger partnerships' (2001). Practitioners also seem to hold a touching faith in partnerships. In their survey and interviews with 70 practitioners in the field of access, Watt and Paterson (2000) found that partnership was deemed a key solution to pressing widening participation problems. However, analyses of existing patterns of collaboration demonstrate that making partnerships work in practice is extremely difficult, and is subject to multiple logistical, organisational, ideological and economic pressures (see Thomas, Cooper and Quinn 2002). Partnerships are thus posited as 'what works', whilst the evidence of their efficacy is surely questionable. For all these reasons, research into educational partnerships has never been more important.

Deep reflexivity: valorising the ethnographic self in educational fieldwork

It is also important to contextualise some of the ways in which the notion of the reflexive ethnographic self has been valorised in sections of social and educational research, with the caveat that the reflexive is certainly not always recognised or rewarded. There are many interesting examples of writing on this issue (see, for example, Van Maanen 1988, Stacey 1988, Skeggs 1994). I have found three discursive fields particularly useful: the ethnographic self and questions of positioning and embodiment; 'troubling the autobiography of the questions' and related issues of autobiography and rapport; and the notion of working the ruins of ethnography and its dilemmas of knowledge and responsibility.

The ethnographic self: positioning and embodiment

In contrast to the impersonal terms of what works, effectiveness and evidence based practice, in which an objective measure can and should be made, with the researcher as instrument, the notion of the ethnographic self foregrounds the mind, the emotions, and even the body, of the researcher. It regards fieldwork as a two way process in which the positioning of the researcher, in different respects – such as age, race, class, gender, sexuality – impacts upon interpretation and must be recognised and accounted for, and where the fieldwork itself impacts upon the researcher's own ongoing constructions of identity and selfhood:

> Whether or not we choose to *write* about our self and our emotional experiences . . . is not my primary concern . . . what is central . . . is the recognition that fieldwork is personal, emotional and identity *work*.
>
> (Coffey 1999: 1, original emphasis)

Troubling the auto/biography of the questions: autobiography and rapport

Whilst the policy-led agenda presents itself as supremely rational, the concept of troubling the auto/biography of the questions takes us deeper into the research process, into understanding where our questions themselves come from and what they mean to us as researchers. It also foregrounds the complex interrelationship between researcher and researched, and how feelings of identification or antipathy impact upon what can be known:

> . . . for me, at times, fieldwork is best understood as both a socio-emotional as well as a rational economy – full of movements to and against an 'other' which are lived as a complex of empathy, indifference and hostility. Certainly in the case of my own work when it felt like so many of the girls 'could have been me', issues of the 'autobiography of the question' cast their long shadow . . . Saying this is not the same as grounding the project in mindless subjectivism. The move is more about critical subjectivism – reconceptualising rapport sociologically as a relation of desire without conceding it as a guarantor of the truth or indeed as the main substantive focus of any study.
>
> (Hey 2000: 173)

Working the ruins of ethnography: knowing and responsibility

The policy-led arena is wedded to certainty and to the finding of the right answer, but reflexive researchers are eternally aware of what they do not and cannot know. However, they are simultaneously conscious of a personal responsibility to counter simplistic pictures, to mobilise what understandings they *can* come to and never be satisfied with the fatuous, the 'common sense' and the 'self evident':

> It is this drawing close . . . that has long been the seduction of fieldwork. This closeness to the practical ways people enact their lives has been the promise for understanding how the everyday gets assumed. The reflexive turn has broadened such understanding to include the very space of ethnographic knowing. Hence to situate ethnography as a ruin/rune is to foreground the limits and necessary misfirings of its assignment . . . The task is to meet the limit, to open to it as the very vitality and force that propels the change to come . . . Attempting to be accountable to complexity, thinking the limit becomes the task, and much opens up in terms of ways to proceed for those who know both too much and too little.
>
> (Lather 2001: 202)

In all the important and, to me, inspiring writing about fieldwork that I have quoted, some common misconceptions about reflexivity are countered. Being reflexive does not necessarily mean writing about yourself; reflexivity does not mean claiming you know something because you 'feel' it; and reflexivity need not mean being defeatist about the limits of what you can claim to know. The arguments of Coffey, Hey and Lather are not outré or egotistical, but eminently thoughtful and responsible, demanding above all that the researcher is aware of all the factors which help construct and delimit what they produce as 'knowledge'. Moreover, although they refer specifically to ethnography, such concepts may apply to any fieldwork in which knowledge is constructed through interpersonal relationships of researcher and participants, and although they may be thrown in sharper relief in their feminist work on girls' friendship or women living with HIV and AIDS, there is no reason why they should not apply to less emotive subjects such as educational partnerships. In fact to bring those two worlds of deep reflexivity and high policy together is what particularly interests me about this piece.

The functionality of the hired hand: researching 'effectiveness'

Lather positions herself as working 'an ethnography of ruins and failures' (2001: 201). The landscape of the HEFCE research I discuss here appears to bear little resemblance to that charted by Lather. It is one where fragmentation and the admission of limitation and failure are not to be born. Whilst one could hardly argue that it is more serious, it certainly seems more solemn. The goal of the research we tendered for, selling ourselves, of course, within the terms of the tender, was to perform an 'evidence based review' of 25 HEFCE funded regional partnerships designed to improve progression to HE for students from disadvantaged backgrounds. The partnerships consisted of universities, colleges of Higher Education and Further Education colleges, combined in varied permutations in an attempt to widen participation. The goal of the research was to establish 'the effectiveness of collaboration strategies in increasing participation in higher education.' Essentially it was a form of policy self-monitoring: have these projects, in which we have invested large sums of funding, worked? It also sought a maximisation of benefits: how can we take what these partnerships have learned and spread it more widely?

It is immediately apparent that the research is couched within the frame of 'what works' and best practice', a frame which has been critiqued as an apparently non-coercive means of securing the effects of power (Atkinson 2000d). Implicit in such an approach is an ultimate goal of application rather than reflection, and a belief that useful judgements can and should be made by those with a claim to expertise. The interesting question, examined in more detail in *Inside the Box* (Quinn, forthcoming), is whether this agenda defines not only the partnerships but how they can be thought about by researchers both within and outside the projects. Within the hired hand loop, is it ever possible to break free of the functional? The expert is hired to do a certain job within a certain institutionalised frame of reference. The agenda of the ethnographic self, which implies certain researcher-directed ethical and epistemological choices, is hardly a priority. How possible is it to move beyond the functional and into the more rarified zone of the socio-emotional, for example? These questions underpin the reflection on this research which forms the rest of this chapter.

Reflecting on an unreflexive process: unpicking the research on educational partnerships

It is quite difficult to reflect on what was fundamentally an unreflexive process but I will attempt to understand what was missing in the partnership research and the implications of this. To outline the research: it consisted of a survey of the twenty-five partnerships, followed by case studies of eight partnerships which were diverse both geographically and in terms of the initiatives they had developed. Within the case studies, which took place over several days for each partnership, members of the research team interviewed those involved in the partnerships, such as Chairs, Steering Group members, Advisory group members, administrators, researchers and project workers. They studied documentation, and sometimes observed meetings and open days. There were four researchers in the research team. I had a key role in four case studies, in transcribing tapes, analysing the themes and co-writing the report. My main impression of the time was of frenzied activity as we struggled to fit in the work alongside other tasks and priorities. To say we never stopped and thought what we were doing would be false; we discussed our goals, even changed direction significantly, but the kinds of questions raised by Coffey (1999), Hey (2000) and Lather (2001), questions about ourselves as researchers, as well as about positioning, autobiography and responsibility, were not on the agenda. The team had a variety of orientations and research predispositions, but if such a call for reflexivity was to be expected, the onus was on me, as a researcher with a particular interest in this area.

Now, revisiting the project, and speaking only for myself, I need to ask: what kinds of questions did I leave out, and what were the consequences of these omissions? I have narrowed the discussion to six questions that might be seen as essential to a reflexive project. These are not 'the questions that shut down the trouble' (Britzman and Dippo 2000: 32), but rather the ones that open it up:

Positioning/Embodiment

How am I positioned, what identity work is happening within this research?

What is the relation between my embodiment and this research?

Autobiography/Rapport

Why am I asking these particular questions and what do they mean to me?

What is my response to the 'others' I am researching?

Knowledge/ Responsibility

How can I think the limits of what I can know through this research?

How can I be accountable to the complexity the research reveals?

Retrospective reflexivity will always be a limited project but having asked these questions I can now start to think about the partnership research in a different way.

Positioning/Embodiment

The answers to my questions are revealing. In terms of positioning and identity work, I can see that the transitions I referred to at the opening of this chapter were important elements in the research process. This was my first hired hand project post PhD, although I had been involved in other research projects without the title of 'Doctor'. Although as a PhD student I had been very conscious of being female, white, older, a mother, just marginally middle class, as a Doctor and external expert it was as if I expected suddenly to transcend these positions. Part of my identity work, my ethnographic self-hood, was proving myself as an accredited 'expert' who was operating with authority beyond selfhood. Much of the negotiation within the research was about power: power to have access to information; power to judge; power to seem in charge. However, at the same time there were elements of embodiment, related in particular to lack of physical energy and to dress code uncertainty, which dogged certain parts of the research, making some case studies seem more 'successful' than others; and this embodiment was, of course, intrinsically linked to the positions I strove to deny.

When I experienced myself as powerful, a sense that increased as the research progressed and as the role of performing Doctor became more familiar, I felt more in tune with the partnerships and perceived them as more coherent and integrated. When my power felt fragmented and dispersed, I seemed more alert to these factors in the partnerships themselves. Whether operating in a comfort zone of skill and physical and mental ease encouraged me to interpret some of the partnerships as exemplifying better practice than others was not explored. Is best practice after all simply what we feel comfortable with? It is possible to see the judgements that I made, not as neutral, but as tied up with a validation of the self as researcher. Had I kept a research diary, as I had so assiduously during my PhD, such factors would have been revealed and their impact on the research finely calculated. I might even have been able to operationalise my multiple positions, rather than pretend they did not exist. And the research would surely have been the richer for it.

Autobiography/Rapport

When it comes to troubling the autobiography of the questions, I can only say that at first there was an artificial insemination by committee. As a group of researchers, we agreed a common set of questions, determined ultimately by the HEFCE agenda, which seem characterised, on reflection, by their impersonality and a formulaic quality. Looking back, what the questions meant to me was imposing order on myself, as much as anything. As such they seem rather uncomfortably tight fitting. They epitomised a rational and, one could argue, reductive view of partnerships: the reality was certainly more messy than this frame allowed. The questions concentrated on structures and organisational frameworks because that was how partnerships were envisaged within the policy discourse, a neat solution where resources and expertise were formally shared. Yet partnerships are not like that: on a negative level they are about how knowledge is blocked or re-routed, to the advantage of the most powerful; in a more positive sense they are also about informal networks and operationalising local knowledges. Our official questions did not lend themselves easily to this understanding, although they did not block it altogether. Not surprisingly, we did not stick rigidly to these questions whilst doing fieldwork, and it was when we departed from them that the research came most alive for me. When I started to ask awkward questions, for example why key decisions were referred to informal meetings between the Chair and his deputy, rather than decided at full meetings, I was able to draw on unofficial knowledge drawn from bitter experience in local authorities:

> *JQ: The Steering Group seems very democratic, but I was interested in the meetings you set up outside it. Is that where the real decisions are made?*
>
> *Chair: You've got a very suspicious mind.*

Reflecting on where such questions came from and why they were important, I was able to see that much of what went on in partnerships was lobbying, power mongering, wheels within wheels. Freeing myself up to ask those meaningful questions opened the box and let some untidy truths drop out.

The question of rapport was an interesting one when researching a diverse group of people, some much more powerful than myself, some with less status, but all of whom had to assign me the authority to make judgements on their work. I was aware of trying to negotiate relationships, developing trust to overcome situations where participants were sometimes very nervous or uncomfortable, being more challenging with the avuncular public figures who always had a smooth story to tell. However, in analysing transcripts none of this delicate balancing was really addressed, unlike my PhD where every sigh and tone was acknowledged. Rapport can be about understanding what is not said, what cannot be said, what is said underneath the words. Why were some of the people we interviewed particularly suspicious and difficult? At the time, the priority seemed to be managing the surly FE lecturer or the monosyllabic researcher so they might relax, feel rapport with us and give us what *we* wanted. However, a more reflexive approach might question why they do not want to speak and what they fear. It might identify silence as a legitimate response for those like the FE lecturer who felt estranged and manipulated within the partnership, as a representative of the Cinderella sector:

> *When they suggested the admin officer should be two people, I said it should be a divorced couple, to epitomise the relationship between HE and FE.*
>
> FE representative, Advisory Group

Silence might also seem a viable strategy for those like the partnership researcher whose role was centralised and subject to strong surveillance from the Chair, and whose research work was seen as justifying the partnership. Control was the essence of this particular game and was not to be easily handed over:

> *. . . the research gives a reason for the whole project . . . It keeps it in a box, a neat package.*
>
> Partnership Project Officer

The research relationships with our participants in some senses mirrored the balancing acts going on in the partnership. Far from being outside the partnership, parachuting down to make judgements, we were highly implicated and enmeshed within it. Since partnerships are really about delicate balancing acts of power, this aspect of the research process might have borne much fruit, had it been addressed more closely.

Knowledge/Responsibility

In probing the limits of what I can know through this research, further questions arise about what I am being allowed or encouraged to know. On the one hand, policy research implies a position of mastery, of knowability, which is at odds with the reflexive turn. Does HEFCE permit Denzin's sixth moment (1997) of reflexive texts which are 'messy, subjective, open ended, conflictual and feminist influenced' (Denzin and Lincoln 1994: 559)? Does it allow the researchers it employs not to know? Conversely, the very notion that experts can come from outside, to apply a generalised judgement to what are local and contingent issues, might be seen as contrary to the postmodernist notions of knowledge production espoused by writers such as Lather. In other words, does this research methodology invalidate any knowledge claims the research might legitimately make?

If one is trying to account for postmodern complexity, then the tools of 'best practice' research are possibly prehistoric. In fact, as I have suggested, a reflexive view of this partnership research reveals notions of objectivity and distance as inherently unworkable in practice. One cannot enter into any research situation without being implicated in the processes one is researching. In researching partnerships, one needs to attend very closely to the chain of power and where the research is positioned within it: who is the partner hub that you must approach to set up your research, who do they lead you to, who can be spoken to, who is unavailable, who speaks eagerly, who is guarded? Who do you represent? Not yourself as ethical researcher operating in the causes of truth and justice, but an immensely powerful funding body, with the authority to dissolve partnerships and with them, jobs and livelihoods. Looking for neutrality and objectivity in this situation is somewhat delusional. Perhaps asking these questions before, not after, the research would have encouraged an alternative methodology with fewer pretensions to objectivity, at least one which was more participative or peer led. However, the question remains: with HEFCE's time frames and priorities would complex and uncertain postmodern knowledge be permissible?

The role of reflexivity in policy research: necessity or luxury?

Is reflexivity, then, a necessity or a luxury? The answer seems surprisingly obvious. It is clear to me that a reflexive approach would have afforded methodological and epistemological benefits to the partnership research. Had I asked the questions which someone committed to reflexivity should have asked, the rewards could have been multiple, and surprisingly tangible. These would have included: a more alert and critical evaluation of what might be interpreted as good practice; greater openness to the messy, non rational aspects of partnerships; greater attention to the importance of delicate balancing acts of power within partnerships; and a methodology more responsive to the local and the situated. None of these understandings would have been impossible to accommodate within the HEFCE frame and all of them would have added depth to the report.

Doing the research would have been different, but not so different as to make it impossible within the time allowed. Indeed, attention to these issues would have made the work less stressful and more intellectually rewarding. Negotiating ways of addressing them as a team, rather than as an individual researcher, would have been more complex, but would have added greater richness to the findings.

Ultimately it seems the ethnographic self is not an academic free loader, but someone who really understands the process and the practicalities of research. However, although reflexivity can add depth, subtlety and methodological finesse, as I have indicated, the ultimate consequence of reflexivity would be to question the terms of the research and, crucially, what was being researched. Reflexivity would have raised some troubling questions about the mechanistic goals of 50% participation. It would also have queried the possibility of partnerships bringing real change into a system which has yet to realise the implications of access in challenging what can and should be known in Higher Education (see Quinn 2001). These questions are the crucial ones when policy-makers are on the brink of making partnership the cornerstone of their widening participation strategy; thus, reflexivity would have fulfilled a vital function in problematising the dominant policy agenda.

If reflexivity is a necessity, albeit a dangerous one, was our research, which was very well received by both HEFCE and the partnerships involved, invalidated by its lack of reflexivity? At a certain level I believe that it did make unwarranted claims of authority that I find highly problematic and, ultimately, it did not allow itself to ask the really important questions. At another level, it did the task it was set to do,within policy terms as currently defined, and, as such, it was perfectly appropriate and fit for purpose. It was a 'good' report. The fundamental question is how can we reconceptualise policy so that it can recognise and utilise more reflexive research?

Conclusion: conjoining reflexivity and educational policy

How possible is it to make policy led research more reflexive? Given the prospective levels of funding suggested by the recent HEFCE Partnerships for Progression consultation, it is clear that the type of research project discussed in this chapter is tied to both large sums of money and significant claims to educational priority. Little wonder then, that the discourses of best practice seem to edge out those of the ethnographic self. However, as Atkinson argues, 'a narrow focus on 'what works' will close the door that leads to new possibilities, new strategies, new ways of reframing and reconceiving the educational enterprise' (2000d: 328). Partnership work is supposed to typify such new strategies and embody a broader perspective on widening participation. A narrow research focus on 'what works' is thus fundamentally inappropriate. If collaboration is a new way to work, then old measures of evaluation cannot encompass it. Making explicit this connection between methodological innovation and innovative policy is the best lever at our disposal to help policy-makers understand the benefits of reflexive research.

Realistically, research on educational policy will not become more reflexive by government dictat, but commitment by researchers to reflexive practice can and must change the way the educational enterprise is understood. Just as feminist analyses of violence against women once considered outrageous have permeated both popular understanding and public policy, so the reflexive turn can potentially transform educational conceptions. This can only happen with a concomitant level of intellectual and emotional investment; only with a transformative vision informed by a rigorous attention to the researcher as self. As researchers, we are always conscious of the limits on our power, and those limits are very real. It may even seem that abandoning ourselves to the doctrine of 'what works' is the only realistic choice:

> For the quickest route to funds and fame has always been sucking up to the establishment, even becoming part of the educational establishment. Hedges and trimmer always proliferate in such closely patrolled circumstances as exist in a small crowded island.
>
> (Goodson 1999: 291)

However, we *do* have powers, as Lather (2001) says, to 'think the limit;' to push at it in our theorising and our practice. These powers should not suddenly desert us when we are recruited to ride as hired hands. In fact, it is all the more important that we hold on to them, leaping over the well trimmed hedges to make a claim on this strategically vital land.

7

The Myth of Mentor as a Double Régime of Truth: Producing docility and devotion in engagement mentoring with 'disaffected' youth

HELEN COLLEY

Helen Colley exposes the myth of mentoring through a combined attack on both its origins and its current interpretations. She takes apart the discourses of caring and control which pervade mentoring, echoing Hursh's concern with the deconstruction of policy rhetoric, while her analysis of the emotional labour inherent in the mentoring model links with Hayes' critique of education as therapy. Her chapter, like those of Quinn and Atkinson, focuses on questions of power and resistance, and on the refusal to be bound by régimes of truth.

Introduction

The last 20 years has witnessed a spectacular growth in the use of mentoring internationally and across a range of contexts. Mentoring has become a central element of initial training and professional development in business management, nursing, teaching, career guidance and many other spheres as well as highly popular as an intervention with young people. This chapter addresses that phenomenon, and argues that a distinctive model – engagement mentoring – has emerged as a response to social exclusion. Here, I interrogate the discourses that surround engagement mentoring, challenging from a critical class and feminist perspective the celebratory mood of the current mentoring movement. (Many of these issues are also relevant to mentoring and ethnic minorities, addressed by Forbes 2000, Gulam and Zulfiqar 1998, and Majors, Wilkinson and Gulam 2000, but that is not the focus of this chapter.)

Discourse, particularly in relation to social exclusion, has been shown to be extremely powerful in shaping social policy and practice, and consequently in shaping material conditions for oppressed groups (Levitas 1996, Marston 2000). In particular, I wish to examine how discourses of mentoring construct both the mentee and the mentor as objects of a process, from the point of view of class and gender. In doing so, I seek to bring questions of power to the fore, and in particular to consider the power dynamics of dyadic mentoring relationships in a way that insists upon their broader contextualisation.

Youth mentoring: a rapid expansion

Mentoring is usually defined as the provision of advice, training, and/or counselling by an experienced person to a junior or novice, through a relatively informal, dyadic relationship. As an education or welfare intervention with young people, Miller (2002) has recently catalogued its expansion on a global scale, claiming that there are now more than 7500 youth mentoring programmes world-wide. One of the most prominent is the Big Brothers Big Sisters (BBBS) movement in the US, which organises hundreds of thousands of mainly white, middle-class volunteers to mentor disadvantaged urban youth. This model has been taken up in Canada and Australia, and in Britain by the Department for Health. Another similar model recruits university students to mentor 'disaffected' young people from poor families. The GEAR-UP programme in the US already organises 1.5 million students in this way. Israel, Sweden and Britain have implemented similar programmes. In addition, many more undergraduates are involved in smaller local projects across Britain, as well as through a raft of national mentoring initiatives that have burgeoned since the election of the Labour government in 1997.

The National Mentoring Network acts as a co-ordinating forum for such initiatives, and has grown from 350 to 1250 members in the last four years, about one third of which are located in post-compulsory education and training. The Network is heavily funded by special bursaries from the Department for Education and Skills (DfES)[1] and most recently by corporate sponsorship from the McDonalds fast food chain. In 1998, the House of Commons Select Committee on Disaffected Children recommended the use of mentoring in all programmes seeking to tackle disaffection. It has since been promoted by four different government departments, covering education and employment, youth justice, health promotion, ethnic minorities, and social exclusion. In January 2001, Gordon Brown, Chancellor of the Exchequer, announced £5.3 million of additional government funding to support the development of such initiatives.

One third of all schools in Britain now use mentoring, and over 750,000 volunteer mentors are active in this way via 2000 different organisations. Some of these are drawn from businesses through 'industrial' mentoring projects, aimed at pupils in their final year of compulsory schooling who are targeted as 'borderline' cases for passing their GCSE exams (Golden and Sims 1997). Others are involved through two major new government initiatives: *Excellence in Cities*, aimed at improving the academic performance of children from disadvantaged communities in inner city schools; and the *Connexions* service, a new national initiative which will replace the existing careers services in England. The aim of *Connexions* is to support young people aged 13–19 through the transitions from adolescence to adulthood and from school to post-compulsory education, training and employment. These programmes rely on volunteers as well as full-time paid mentors. *Excellence in Cities* and *Connexions* have already employed 2400 learning mentors in schools in their first two years of operation, and this is set to rise to 3000 over the next two years. In addition, *Connexions* is seeking to recruit and train 20,000 personal advisers to work in mentorship roles with 16–19 year-olds.

Engagement mentoring: a new model

An extensive review of these developments (discussed more fully in Colley 2003 and forthcoming) reveals that a distinctive new model of mentoring has emerged over the last decade. I term this 'engagement mentoring'. Engagement mentoring differs from the model of industrial mentoring in schools which specifically avoids involving socially excluded young people, since they might prove unreliable or intractable in meetings with mentors, and schools are reluctant to alienate the business people who volunteer (Golden and Sims 1997). It is also distinct from the model of 'community' or 'positive action' mentoring, which seeks to help young people from ethnic minorities overcome the discriminatory barriers they face (Forbes 2000, Miller 2002, Skinner and Fleming 1999). A third distinction can be drawn, as it differs again from the mentoring role traditionally undertaken by youth workers, linked to the process of informal education, and firmly centred on and negotiated around the needs and interests of the young person (Philip and Hendry 1996).

Engagement mentoring has a number of defining characteristics which link it to 'welfare-to-work' policies (cf. Freedman 1999). It is planned and formalised within institutional settings and agendas. It is targeted specifically at socially excluded young people, often in the period following compulsory schooling, and its aim is to re-engage such young people with the formal labour market and structured routes thereto. Moreover, legal and financial compulsion to participate is often an element, e.g. benefit payments may be withdrawn, hostel accommodation terminated, or probation replaced by imprisonment if the young person does not comply.

Yet despite its phenomenal expansion, mentoring in general, and engagement mentoring in particular, remains weakly conceptualised, under-researched and under-theorised (Colley 2001a, 2001b, Piper and Piper 2000, Roberts 2000a, 2000b). There is, moreover, little evidence to support its use as an intervention with socially excluded young people (Skinner and Fleming 1999), and its popularity is not matched by critical understanding that might inform policy and practice. Above all, the dyadic nature of the mentoring relationship has encouraged narrowly individualised perspectives upon the subject. Research in the field is dominated by the discipline of psychology, and by quantitative survey and statistical approaches. As a result, mentoring is almost invariably disembedded from its social, economic and political context (Gulam and Zulfiqar 1998), and it is this decontextualisation that I challenge.

Firstly, I review the way in which power has been represented in academic discourses of mentoring. Since the scope of the available literature on engagement mentoring is very limited, consisting overwhelmingly of short-term, small-scale evaluation reports, this brief review draws on research and writing from a range of contexts in addition to the specific field of engagement mentoring. I then take the case of engagement mentoring, and analyse in turn its discourse in relation to the young people who are targeted as mentees, and the discourse which seeks to construct mentors' roles in a particular way. Finally, I link these two discourses to argue that they represent parallel elements of a double régime of truth.

Mentoring and power

Power has always been central to academic discussions of mentoring, though with differing degrees of transparency. The operation of power is a fundamental assumption of the traditional, 'classic' model of mentoring. According to this model, an older, more experienced and powerful mentor supports a less experienced junior in establishing their career. It is most common in the literature on business management, but also informs many people's everyday understanding of mentoring. The developmental psychology studies which first brought mentoring to prominence, such as Levinson's seminal work, *The Seasons of a Man's Life* (Levinson *et al* 1978), reify power as a commodity that is handed over from senior to novice in a kind of zero-sum equation. As knowledge, experience and authority gradually equalise in the balance between mentor and mentee, the two are drawn into peer status, and the balance then tips in favour of the younger person, as the older partner goes into decline and heads for retirement.

Despite acknowledging that women (Kram 1988) and working class men (Levinson *et al* 1978) tended to be excluded from this process of mentoring as sponsorship, the operation of power within mentoring relationships is treated as highly individualised in this model. Mentees are portrayed, predominantly, as passive recipients of mentor support, as those whose deficits are 'topped up' through mentoring to allow them to function eventually with autonomy. This individualised psychological view is maintained in the few studies which identify the 'dark side of mentoring' (Long 1997, see also Scandura, 1998). Damaging consequences are thus usually attributed to the abuse of power by mentors.

This view of power changed, however, as mentoring became formalised in a range of professional development contexts. In the

1980s, as economic competitiveness sharpened, businesses replaced traditional forms of training and development with mentoring. This trend was intensified by the de-layering of businesses, with the removal of personnel development staff and middle managers who would previously have taken some responsibility for training needs (Megginson and Clutterbuck 1995). Other political developments ushered in mentoring elsewhere. Competency-based approaches favoured the use of mentors in professional training in nursing, career guidance, social work and other public services. In teaching, political decisions shifted initial teacher education away from Higher Education institutions and into schools (Gay and Stephenson 1998, Stammers 1992). This created some concerns about the way in which supposedly dyadic relationships were being opened up to the intrusion of institutional goals and agendas. The process of mentoring became linked to the process of formal assessment, for example. In contexts like teaching, where professional roles and competencies were ever more prescribed, mentors were ascribed a gate-keeping function linked to assessment, in addition to their supportive, developmental role.

Emerging critical analyses located mentoring relationships along a spectrum of power that ranges from hierarchy to reciprocity, from controlling to empowering, and from directive to non-directive (Gay and Stephenson 1998). Within teaching and nursing in particular, such issues of power have become linked with that of gender. A number of liberal feminist authors have taken up themes which counterpose concepts of asymmetry and nurture to those of hierarchy and control in mentoring relationships (Standing 1999). They argue that even all-female dyads in these contexts fall into the 'classic' model with its assumptions of paternalism and male patterns of psychological development on the part of the mentor. A liberal feminist model of mentoring would be based on concerns for reciprocity, solidarity and empowerment between partners, and that these represent 'women's ways' of collaborating that might escape the oppressive conditions of patriarchal relationships (DeMarco 1993, Cochran-Smith and Paris 1995).

These critiques, however, continue to indicate that responsibility for the character of mentoring lies with the mentors, and that the mentees are essentially vulnerable, particularly where their status is marginalised by class, ethnic origin or gender. But, although critiques recognise the *triadic* nature of relationships between mentor, mentee, and dominant external groups, they do not explore fully the implications of this triad. They retain an individualised view of how power operates within the mentoring dyad itself. The significance of institutional intrusion into the dyad is discussed predominantly as increasing the power and authority of the mentor over the mentee (as where the mentor has a role in formal assessment), therefore creating greater potential for abuses of that power.

In reviewing this literature, two issues began to strike me as worthy of further investigation. The first was that there seemed to be a further rationale for the term 'engagement mentoring', beyond its mission to re-engage young people with the labour market. Over and over again, reports of these projects referred to their aim of altering young people's attitudes, values and beliefs in order to make them employable. This seemed to indicate an effort to engage their 'hearts and minds' with the aspirations of their prospective employers, in a way that obscured more fundamental oppositions of interests between workers and those who own the means of production.

The second was that the vast majority of professional and volunteer mentors working with socially excluded youth are women, as are most mentors in nursing, primary teaching, career guidance etc. Social gender constructions stereotypically represent the role of women as carers and nurturers, both within the family and in paid work. This is part of women's oppression within patriarchal society. From this point of view, the problem may be seen not so much as that of female mentors unwittingly embracing male forms of domination and control. Rather, it indicates that promoting a discourse of *nurture* for mentoring is not itself unproblematic for those who act as mentors. Utilising these two perspectives, I look at how dominant discourse constructs the identities of both mentees and mentors within engagement mentoring.

Engagement mentoring: the production of docility in mentees

Although in part inspired by developments in the US, the major impetus for the growth of engagement mentoring in the UK came from the Youthstart Initiative, a strand of the European Social Fund which sought to address the problem of youth unemployment. Youth-start funded over 70 projects across the UK from 1994–1999, and its policy guidelines encouraged the use of mentoring as a central aspect of their work. Twenty of these projects were located in careers services, co-ordinated into a national Mentoring Action Project (MAP) by the Institute of Career Guidance (ICG). The significance of the MAP cannot be underestimated. Not only did it form the largest engagement mentoring project in Britain until that time, but in many respects it went on to form a pilot for the new *Connexions* youth support service.

European policy for the Youthstart Initiative proposed mentoring as part of a 'comprehensive pathway' approach to re-engage young people with the labour market. Each stage of this pathway

> . . . is associated with bringing about a *significant shift in the values and motivation* of the young people, their skills and abilities and in their interaction with the wider environment. The overall objective is to move the young person from a position of alienation and distance from social and economic reality, to a position of social integration and productive activity.
> (European Commission 1998: 6, emphasis added)

The purpose of mentoring was specified as being

> . . . to reinforce *the acceptance of values and attitudinal change amongst the young people.*
> (European Commission 1998: 12, emphasis added)

Apart from questioning the assumption that engaging further with the 'social and economic realities' of the labour market does not itself involve alienation, one might ask *whose* values and *which* attitudes are to be promoted. The evaluation of mentoring within the British Youthstart projects suggests an answer, defining part of the mentors' role thus

> [to] endorse the work ethic, and . . . challenge any negative percep-tions the young person may have about entry to the labour market
> (Employment Support Unit 2000: 7)

The MAP subscribed to this approach:

> the mentors' primary task of *influencing behaviours, and by impli-cation attitudes*, is a fundamental one
> (Ford 1999: 18, emphasis added)

It is no surprise that this is a recurrent theme. The Labour government's report *Bridging the Gap* (Social Exclusion Unit 1999) offers the same analysis. It argues that the key barriers to young people's engagement with the labour market are their own attitudes, values, beliefs and behaviour, and that the primary task of transition 'support' should be to alter those dispositions (see Colley and Hodkinson 2001 for a fuller critique).

These discourses have impacted considerably upon the way in which young people's transitions beyond compulsory schooling are understood and interpreted for young people themselves by agencies guiding them through those transitions: careers services, schools, colleges and training providers. I have argued elsewhere (Colley 2000b) that a major shift has occurred in contemporary accounts of career transitions through the dominance of a particular, triumphalist discourse of globalisation. This shift promotes three common themes: firstly, that labour market entrants should accept insecurity, intensified productivity, poor working conditions and low wages in a climate of global competitiveness; secondly, that guidance should help clients re-invent their own identities as marketable products, particularly through commitment to their employers' interests; and thirdly, that practitioners' main role is to overcome young people's resistant attitudes to these demands. But what are the attitudes, values, behaviours and beliefs that engagement mentoring is supposed to foster in young people?

Numerous policy documents and research reports present a similar picture (e.g. DfEE 2000a, 2001, Glynn and Nairne 2000), but the report *Towards Employability* by the employers' organisation Industry in Education (1996) offers perhaps the starkest presentation. This report emphasises employers' demands for 'compromise and respect' in young workers (p9); that staff need to 'sign on to the values and ethos of the business and fit into its organisational structure, culture and work ethics . . . to 'go with' the requirements of the job' (p10); and that young people need to consider and adapt 'their own values, attitudes, human interactions' (p10) in line with the interests of the employing organisation. It is not surprising, then, that the requirement for employability in young people has been criticised as having 'more to do with shaping subjectivity, deference and demeanour, than with skill development and citizenship' (Gleeson 1996: 97).

It is for these reasons also – the purpose of re-engaging young people with the formal labour market, *by engaging their personal commitment to meet the demands of employers* – that I have come to refer to mentoring in this context as 'engagement mentoring'. As Maguire, Ball and Macrae argue, current UK policies relating to youth transitions,

> so commonly expressed now in the reductionist terms of the requirements of international economic competitiveness, are almost exclusively concerned with the production of future workers with particular skills *or dispositions* . . . the work ethic and human capital theory generate between them a very utilitarian version of *what it is be a young person* in contemporary society
>
> (2001: 199, emphasis added)

In addition to becoming tied to employment-related outcomes, mentoring for socially excluded young people, whether delivered through *Connexions*, other specific initiatives, or as an element of vocational training, has come to target young people's dispositions – the very heart of what it is to be a person. Instead of responding to and caring for the uniqueness of each individual, as the rhetoric of mentoring would have us believe, it in fact creates a normalising 'gaze', which focuses, but does not centre, upon the individual (cf. Stronach 1989), and demands conformity to a generalised stereotype of the employable young worker.

There is, in one sense, little new about this. Employers' demands for employable young people have been described as 'the long moan of history', reaching back at least a century (Rikowski 2001: 30). However, even the most behaviourist of previous approaches in vocational education and training never posed such a direct mission of intervening in *individual* dispositions through the vehicle of close human relationships, in the way that engagement mentoring does today. One way of understanding this intervention is through Foucault's (1991a) concept of the production of docility, the disciplinary functioning of power upon disposition to create acceptance of the social and economic *status quo* imposed by dominant groupings. But are those who mentor simply agents or accomplices of such a régime? I turn now to the discourses that construct the role of mentors.

The myth of Mentor: the production of devotion in mentors

A seemingly ubiquitous feature of texts about mentoring – policy documents, practitioner guidelines, and academic literature – is the way in which the mentor role is descriptively defined, rhetorically embellished, and ideologically legitimated by reference to Ancient Greek myth (Colley 2001a, 2001b, Roberts 1999, 2000b). The origins of the mentor concept are ritually traced to the character named Mentor in Homer's epic poem, *The Odyssey*. According to this legend, when the king Odysseus left his wife and small son to go and fight in the Trojan war, he entrusted the guardianship of the household and the child to his old and trusted friend, Mentor. Many modern accounts of mentoring focus on the figure of Mentor, comparing his surrogate parental role to that of the mentor in the classic model already discussed. However, other authors identify that it is not Mentor himself, but the goddess Athene (albeit at times in the guise of Mentor) who represents the key figure in the mentoring of Odysseus' son, as described by Homer.

One typical evocation of the mentor as Athene can be found in the Mentoring Action Project (MAP) report (Ford 1999), which, as we have seen, has been highly influential in the evolution of engagement mentoring in the UK. A whole section of the report's preface, which aims to clarify the terminology used, includes this description of the ethos of mentoring:

> It is illuminating to return to the original source of the word 'mentor', and to discern at least some of the characteristics of behaviour which lent force to the term entering the English language in order to describe *a particular quality of caring relationship*.
>
> (Ford 1999: 9, emphasis added)

In describing the female deity Athene, Ford emphasises her 'specialness', her inspirational character, and her dedication and self-sacrifice to meet the needs of Odysseus' son. The mentor's role is described as 'selfless caring' (p8) and 'selfless giving' (p14), 'caring for each individual client, which was warm, dispassionate, spontaneous and non-judgemental, and with a readiness to go that 'additional mile' beyond the call of duty' (p13). These themes are echoed in numerous other texts, all using the image of Athene to present powerful visions of mentors as saintly and self-sacrificing in their devotion to their mentee. At the same time, as I have shown in the parallel discourse about the goals of mentoring for socially excluded young people, mentors are represented as almost super-human in their power to transform mentees.

These happy modern renditions in fact bear little resemblance to Homer's bloody and brutal tale of military, economic, political and sexual conquest by the king and his son on Odysseus' return home, and I have offered elsewhere a socialist feminist analysis of the gulf between the actual story of mentoring originally told in *The Odyssey* and its modern simulacra (Colley 2001a, 2002). Of interest here, however, is the fact that the vision of Athene-as-Mentor is an image central to the appeal made by the liberal feminists (e.g. Cochran-Smith and Paris 1995, DeMarco 1993, Standing 1999). As a goddess, Athene is held up as a role model of a powerful woman, as the fount of wisdom, and as a champion of other women. Yet nothing could be further from the purpose her image served in Ancient Greece, and we need to look much more closely at the symbolism of that time. According to legend, Athene had no mother, but burst forth from the head of Zeus, king of the gods. Thus her birth symbolised both the violent termination of the earlier matrilineage and the triumph of male rationality. This was a society on the cusp of social upheaval, and such a legend served to consolidate the nascent patriarchal power (which went hand in hand with class divisions and the appropriation of the means of production) and to stave off the threat still posed by the recently defeated matriarchy (Reed 1975). Athene may have a female form, but in Greek mythology she represents a surrogate for male interests and domination.

In a similar way, the use of Athene, even by feminists, in current discourses of mentoring is also something of an unwitting vehicle for the interests of patriarchal, capitalist interests. Just as the discourse around mentees demands a transformation of their disposition, so too engagement mentoring demands a transformation of disposition in the mentor. She is not only supposed to manage her own feelings to display devotion and kindly nurture towards the mentee, but she is also supposed to present an ideal role model of the employable worker, and of rational action within the normative framework dictated by employers' needs. Such a discourse exacts a process of emotional labour (Hochschild, 1983), which impacts disproportion-ately on women given their lower social status, and produces expecta-tions that they will act out simultaneously the 'two leading roles of Womanhood' (Hochschild 1983: 175): maternal caring for the needs of others and professional distance and control.

If we equate reciprocity, solidarity and the neutralisation of power within the mentoring dyad with liberation and empowerment, we deny the invisible and normative operation of more subtle forms of power, which work not only against the mentee, but against the mentor too through deep-rooted structures of gender oppression in our society (cf. Walkerdine 1992). By focusing on the power of the mentor and the powerlessness of the mentee, liberal feminist critiques of mentoring deny powerlessness for the mentor, and pathologise oppression *for both mentor and mentee*. Within the nurturing model of mentoring, the mentor bears heavy personal costs as she tries to create the 'ideal', 'employable' young person out of the 'disaffected' (see Hulbert 2000 for early empirical evidence of the negative impact of such work on personal advisers in careers services and *Connexions* pilots). Mentoring becomes a 'technology of the self' (Foucault 1988), which promotes self-less dedication to the client without any critical understanding of the social relations in which the relationship is placed. In reforming her own disposition to model an idealised embodiment of rational, normative behaviour, the mentor is entrapped in an act of violence against herself that goes beyond the symbolic. This brings me to draw together the parallel discourses of both mentor and mentee.

A double régime of truth

It is common in our society to use a discourse of intimate voluntary and biological human bonds to represent shallower relationships that are in fact only legal and artificial (Almond 1991). Engagement mentoring may be a prime example of this tendency, with its promise of freedom from social exclusion through the formation of a close personal relationship, so often represented in the language of parent-ing or of an older sibling (as in 'Big Brothers Big Sisters'). But when the institutional masquerades as the personal, we have to ask whether having such a policy for social inclusion constitutes a promise or a threat (cf. Wickert 1997). Are these *ersatz* relationships offering vulnerable young people 'a stone in exchange for bread' (Almond 1991: 71)? And what are the reciprocal implications for mentors labouring under the expectation of idealised role models?

I have made two arguments central to this chapter. The first is that engagement mentoring seeks to engender docility in young mentees through its discourse of reform for 'employability'. The second is that engagement mentoring seeks to engender self-sacrificing devotion in mentors through its discourse of feminine nurture. Such devotion can, of course, be seen as another form of docility, and one that connects with millennia of gender oppression for the majority of mentors who are women. Modern myths of Mentor function as a double régime of truth that imposes specific cultural patterns while also imposing the belief that things were ever thus. The practice of mentoring can thus be seen as a technology of the self for both mentees and mentors, a normalising process in which disciplinary power is both internalised and rendered invisible.

In this regard, while one suspects that the fashion sense of policy is fickle, and may wish to dress itself up in newer initiatives in the future, engagement mentoring nevertheless represents an expression of more enduring tendencies: above all, the individualisation of learning and responsibility for learning. As Ecclestone (1999) has so rightly noted, this represents a moralisation of 'risk', whereby risk is constructed as any kind of non-conformity by those who 'should' be learners. Using the notion of a double régime of truth in engagement mentoring, I would argue that it also represents a *moralisation of care*, in the devotion that is expected from those who are supposed to return recalcitrants to the learning fold.

I have reported in detail elsewhere (Colley 2000a) empirical evidence of the ways in which young people resisted the régime of engagement mentoring. Here, following Gore (1993), I argue that liberating possibilities are offered simply through the act of naming a régime of truth. Naming a discourse can challenge unconscious acceptance of it, and enable resistance to its disciplinary function. As the mentoring juggernaut careers ahead, such critical ways of thinking about its practice are needed to temper the celebratory hype that currently fuels its rampant progress.

Helen Colley

Acknowledgements

I am grateful to Alison Aitken and Suzanne Mather at the National Mentoring Network for their expert help in tracing the latest developments in mentoring.

The research project on which this paper is based was funded by a PhD studentship bursary from the Manchester Metropolitan University. I am indebted to my supervisors Jane Artess, Mary Issitt (both at Manchester Metropolitan University) and Phil Hodkinson (now at the University of Leeds) for their support.

Note

1. The Department for Education and Skills (DfES) was known as the Department for Education and Employment (DfEE) until its restructure after Labour's re-election to a second term in June 2001.

PART TWO

PART TWO

8

The Terror! The Terror! Speaking the Literal to Inspire the Understanding of a Friend

JEROME SATTERTHWAITE

The chapter opens with writing that is self-consciously mannered, allusive and elevated; but that style is then made the subject of critique as an example of academic discourse with which learners are made to come to terms. This is the issue which Burn and Finnigan explore, reminding us of the strenuous process of contest and negotiation by which, Rowland has argued, knowledge is won. The chapter recalls Rowland's debate, suggesting a resolution of the us-and-them of educational discourse by applying Levinas' notion of the 'Other'.

There are a range of ways of reading the title of this chapter. At one end there is what I am going to call, for want of a better name, the naïve, or innocent, reading. Read this way, 'The terror! The terror! Speaking the literal to inspire the understanding of a friend' makes very little sense. It is an oxymoron; but in saying that I will have further complicated the divisions amongst you, the readers of this chapter, setting up what will by now have become four categories: those of you who have not decoded the title's references and also do not know what an oxymoron is, those of you who know what an oxymoron is but have not decoded the title; those who have decoded the title but do not know what an oxymoron is; and finally those, whom we must call the sophisticated readers, who have succeeded in both the little academic tests I have set you so far. But if I now make a wry comment about sophistication, reminding you what Socrates has to say about sophistry and the shallowness of the sophists' pretensions, I shall probably have succeeded in infuriating everyone without exception.[1]

The major reference in the title is to Conrad's *Heart of Darkness*. This short novel was first published in 1902 and rapidly became one of the most influential novels of the 20th Century. The narrator is Marlow, an English seaman who has travelled the world and seen strange sights, but who takes for granted his membership of the civilised, class-bound value system of his day, by which he judges his own and others' behaviour. He tells his tale to four other Englishmen, none of them named or characterised beyond the fact that their leader is referred to as 'The Director of Companies'. They are aboard this man's yacht, waiting for the tide. It is to help them pass the time that Marlow tells them his tale, of a white man who has 'gone native', disappearing into the African jungle, where he has been confronted with a knowledge so alien and so total in its threat to civilised understanding that he, along with Marlow the narrator and the novel as a whole, can only describe it as 'The horror! The horror!'

This is how the novel describes the climactic moment when the central character is confronted with this 'complete knowledge' (Conrad 1994: 99):

> Anything approaching the change that came over his features I have never seen before, and hope never to see again. Oh, I wasn't touched. I was fascinated. It was as though a veil had been rent. I saw on that ivory face the expression of sombre pride, of ruthless power, of craven terror – of an intense and hopeless despair. Did he live his life again in every detail of desire, temptation, and surrender during that supreme moment of complete knowledge? He cried in a whisper at some image, at some vision – he cried out twice, a cry that was no more than a breath: '*The horror! The horror!*'

The reference in the subtitle is to the second stanza of Robert Frost's poem 'Revelation' (Frost 1971: 19). This is, on the face of it, a slight poem, making no large claims for metaphysical or psychological insight. It is taken from Frost's first collection of poems, published in 1913, entitled disarmingly *A Boy's Will*.

The second stanza reads

> 'Tis pity if the case require
> (Or so we say) that in the end
> We speak the literal to inspire
> The understanding of a friend.

These two quotations, concerned with arriving at knowledge or understanding (leaving aside for the time being the issue of what can be claimed for such arrivals), frame the discussion of this chapter. But for the moment I want to stay with the business of references, to look more closely at what is implied, about me the writer and you the reader, in the practice of alluding in this way.

If you decoded the reference to Conrad in the title of this chapter, you may have been intrigued or amused. The fact that Conrad is not quoted but parodied will have been part of the pleasure. You and I have, in effect, shared a nice academic joke. But perhaps your pleasure went further than merely enjoying that sense of being an insider, one of the 'in crowd'; perhaps my title set you thinking. You may have speculated about my turning 'horror' into 'terror'; Eliot's *The Waste Land* or *The Hollow Men* may have come to mind; perhaps *Apocalypse Now*; possibly the discussion of these connections in Michael Woods' recent article in the *London Review of Books*.[2] My title has situated this chapter in the play (playground) of intertextuality; but intertextuality here is another word for cultural capital. The play is between texts readers may be able, however faintly, to call to mind; and this is a function of how 'well read', how rich in cultural capital, the readers may be. Like a smooth guest at an intellectual soirée, my phrase glides about in your mind amongst words and phrases of its kind, acknowledging some prominent connections, but making only the faintest of inclinations towards others, sure of itself in that assembly, out of place and insignificant elsewhere.

This is the way literary allusions work. They define in the terms of whoever makes them what it is to be educated. Whether you are educated or not is determined, in this context, by my choice of allusion: I set the test; you either passed, with or without honours, or failed. On the other hand, as a kind of educational revenge, whether I am educated or not is determined, in this context, by your view of the

105

appositeness, wit and charm of my allusions: are they relevant, smart, up-to-date, suave; or have I dragged them in where they do not properly belong, or paraded them with an indecent flourish, thus betraying intellectual insecurity? These are matters of fine judgement; matters, perhaps, of taste. It seems that the sober and serious business of learning and teaching is inextricably bound up with the conferment or withholding of awards; or perhaps 'rewards' is a better word for the kind of recognition that follows successful accomplishment in this competitive and censorious coterie, where the best any of us can hope for is to belong.

It would be a relief to suppose that this view of education falls away when we turn aside from the game of exchanging cultural references and attend to the more serious business of the transmission and reception of ideas and values which is the central project of education in the humanities and social sciences. The argument of this chapter is that the opposite is the case: that the game of exchanging cultural references goes on, but in a less obvious form, through the use of specialised and rare vocabularies involving similar negotiations between the educator and learner. Suppose I had swiped my title clean of literary allusion, and had instead offered a title made up from the technical vocabulary of philosophy. To take an example more or less at random, suppose I had included in my title the word 'phenomenology'. There are no literary references here. But references no less recondite are innumerable. 'Phenomenology' might recall Husserl or Heidegger, perhaps Sartre or Levinas; or perhaps de Beauvoir, or Gadamer, or Merleau-Ponty. What about Foucault, for that matter, whose *The Order of Things* was, according to Eribon (1991: 157) *inspired and driven by polemics against Husserl's thought and Merleau-Ponty's interpretation of it*. Google[3] found 123,000 references to 'Phenomenology' in 0.1 seconds. The website of the Center for Advanced Research in Phenomenology had been visited 70813 times since March 1997, at the time of writing this chapter. Each visitor will have brought, and carried away, a view of what 'phenomenology' means. But this is merely to scratch the surface of the present state of studies in Phenomenology. Google does not know everything. The word 'phenomenology' is not unlike the word 'Scandinavia', which is the name given to a collection of ten thousand islands, some big, some tiny, some important in terms of trade, others important in terms of geology, others significant for their strategic position, others again for their historical associations: battles that were fought there, chieftains who were wrecked on their rocks. Each of us, confronted by either the word 'phenomenology' or the word 'Scandinavia', will have a more or less imperfect sense of what it means. What is certain is that no one (perhaps not even I myself) will know precisely what I mean when I use these words. There is an important sense in which, when I use words of this kind, nobody knows what I am talking about.[4]

This is an argument for falling silent, in the spirit of Wittgenstein's quasi-mystical injunction: *Whereof one cannot speak, thereof one must be silent.* (Wittgenstein 1922: 189). Wittgenstein is thinking here of the propositions of philosophy, which he thinks strictly unutterable; for him it is only the propositions of the natural sciences that can be put into words; and his view is that they tell us nothing of any serious importance. But education involves speaking beyond the limits of the physical, μέτα τα φυσικά (meta ta phousika, meaning 'beyond the natural/physical'). We are faced with a dilemma: educators speak about education; but to speak about such things is to be misunderstood. This issue is fundamental, having to do with the problems of other minds, of language and of meaning, which are beyond the scope of this chapter. What I want to do here is examine responses to this dilemma. I want to look at why being misunderstood may seem positively attractive to some educators and why some people, including some students, may enjoy not being able to understand what others are talking about. Then I want to question some of the assumptions which may lie behind the act of educative communication, and to suggest alternative assumptions which I think may make education work better.

In the summer of 2001 in the University of Plymouth School of Graduate Studies we asked students on our Cert. Ed. and PGCE PCET courses[5] to tell us about what we called 'long words'. We asked them to tell us 'how certain kinds of word can get in the way of understanding' and we asked them to comment on what they thought was going on when they encountered words they did not understand. Here is a comment from a Cert. Ed. student:

> Throughout the course I have struggled with the language which is very demotivating indeed. . . . It was very disappointing as I felt the

underlying theory to be relevant but it was dressed up in this annoy-
ing, pretentious language. I think that a clever author draws the
reader in by making it simple, interesting and readable!!! . . . I just
don't understand why he has to dress it up in such complex
language. It seems that because he is an 'intellectual', he has to
prove this by writing lots of big, complicated words!

The feeling here is one of anger and frustration. The student feels
humiliated by inability to understand what is being written, but,
equally, thinks the writer is simply showing off. Another student
wrote:

Why do the lecturers on Cert Ed not speak English? We have a
brain but do not need to be impressed! Simple English is more
easily understood than impressive gobbledegook!

Again, the anger is unmistakable. These students saw no merit at all
in the specialised vocabulary of educational theory, and felt resentment towards the writers and lecturers who use it. A more complex
reaction is expressed in this student's comment:

It feels like (as a student) each group has its own club, and as a
student it takes time to absorb this terminology in order to become
a member – as well as confidence to ask if you do not understand in
class, and a good dictionary.

Sometimes it feels as if authors of journals and books deliberately
load the texts with specialised language. I am not sure of the reason
for this. Maybe they want their reader to think more deeply
about the subject; or they want to show their own expertise and
superiority; or they want to be acknowledged as a valid member of
the club?

This comment includes some recognition for the need of specialised
language, and a guarded acknowledgement that it may serve a
purpose. More significantly, this student is aware of a 'club' which
she/he is being invited to join, through the initiating ritual of acquir-
ing the members' specialised discourse.

What is striking about these comments is the implicit recognition of
two kinds of person involved in the processes of education: on the one
hand, the educators, learned, distinguished, constructed as different
by the discourse which defines them; on the other, the unlearned,
seeking learning, humiliated and resentful but at the same time

fascinated by the styles and pretensions of their educators. Students' written responses were saturated with comments, often in brackets, quite often followed by more than one exclamation mark: '(honest!!)', '(Horrid label, I know)', '(or not perhaps)', 'It has made me feel small, stupid, bored and worried!!!', '(If I am right!!!)'. The writers' self-deprecation is clear: these are strong criticisms of academic style, but expressed in the apologetic tones of writers who have not themselves mastered this style, and who are embarrassed and ashamed. Students confident enough to laugh were rare. Here is one example:

> It is rather like those geeks who use specialised language about computers. They are talking amongst themselves. The rest of us experience alienation; and that may be part of what they want to happen.

> You hear a word in a lecture or read it in an article. You look it up in a dictionary and it's not there. Now you're screwed.

'Geeks' and 'screwed' are interesting words here: deliberately disrespectful, they repudiate the discourse by an amused, contemptuous mockery. Another student commented:

> Long words are necessary. They provide a bubble of protection around those who use them, protecting them against criticism/ challenge.

The student quoted earlier recognises the distance alienating her from the academics; but, by an odd twist (which brings her closer to Bourdieu (1991: 54) than he might find easy to imagine), she shares his contempt for the 'philosophers' chatting amongst themselves while the world goes by. She acknowledges her exclusion from the game, putting herself in a category similar to the one I labelled 'naïve' in my opening comment; but her rejection is, in fact, the opposite of naïve: she has no desire to be a 'geek'.

A gentler tone is adopted by another student:

> I agree that there are many words which make reading literature hard work. I find myself adopting the 'opera' approach: you have no understanding of what they are singing about but pick up clues.

The image here is of academics warbling away, engrossed in their passionate but private exchanges; but the comparison captures, too, the suggestion of their being aware of, and playing up to, an audience raptly attentive to the exchanges they cannot properly understand, but which they perceive to be significant and indeed important to the elevated people who utter them. Unlike John Stuart Mill's poets, whom he supposed to be 'utterly unconscious' of a listener,[6] academics, on this view, act out their strangeness before a passive audience who are suitably impressed, and have, indeed, paid to watch the show. Without students' reverent attention, the show would stop. The same student goes on to say

> You also falsely kid yourself that you understand what they are on about just the same as listening to an overheard conversation whilst on holiday.

The sense of exclusion appears again in this comment; but so does the sense that what is overhead is intriguing, offering a glimpse of something about which the listener would like to know more, if only the role of eavesdropper would allow it. In Yorkshire dialect this student would describe herself as 'nebbing', poking her nose into other people's business.

This view of education as the purview of an élite appears consistently throughout the students' responses, as does the perception of teaching/lecturing as performance. One student wrote:

> There's something exciting about the flow of language which you don't understand. It makes you feel that you are on the way to becoming a member of a specially intellectual group. There is something nice, too, about hearing language well used – just for its own sake. The sense of confidence in an academic speaker, and the contributions from the floor which show that he/she has been understood, makes a good impression: you want to be part of this.

This is language perceived as glossalalia, the speaking with tongues about which St Paul had such mixed feelings.[7] The student is impressed by the eloquence of this strange performer, the more so as she cannot understand a word. We notice, again, the sense of insiders' knowledge – the contributions from the floor – which excite this respondent with the sense that she can join this 'specially intellectual group'. She may not know what the speaker is talking about, but there are those who do, and she means to become one of their number. Precisely because she cannot understand it, what is being said has a dignity which sets it apart from ordinary comment. It is something ordinary language would not be competent to express.

Whether they were irritated, resentful or inspired, most students saw themselves as taking part in a quasi-sacred ritual, which it would be impertinent to interrupt. They saw themselves as subordinates, disciples, recognising the remoteness of the discourse of education from the world of their own experience. Whatever they felt about it,[8] they were always aware that the processes of education were about drawing them, the neophytes, into the mystery, the *disciplina arcani,*[9] through the transmission to them from those already initiated of a sacred vocabulary and wordplay. Looking up these words in dictionaries, as the students quickly discovered, was little use. Words of this kind are described in other words of the same kind, clustering, like the relatives of the victim of some brutish attack, about one of their number whose meaning has been rudely demanded, able only to murmur their sympathy amongst themselves.

It is a measure of the power of this discourse that, for the most part, students were prepared to try so painstakingly to learn the language of their educators. Some resisted, as illustrated in the terse comment of one student, that 'One thing you can do with language you don't understand is to use it in an essay as a quote.' Most did not have this confidence, or the insouciance it suggests. For the most part, students' responses showed their earnest commitment to acquire the new vocabulary and the confidence to handle it effectively, which they saw as valuable.

This chapter is similarly unsure of where it stands. The scholarliness – the footnotes, the references to Plato, Wittgenstein, St Paul *et al* (together with phrases such as *et al*, and other little bits of Greek and Latin) – are there to serve two purposes which are, if not at odds, at least in uneasy tension. On the one hand, I want to impress the reader with my learning. This is, after all, an academic chapter, presented in an academic publication for scholarly readers. As such it needs to demonstrate, decorously and with a cool assurance, its academic competence. I do not want the reader sniggering at solecisms (*solecism, n. Offence against grammar or idiom, blunder in the manner of speaking or writing; piece of ill breeding or incorrect behaviour. . . . [f. L f. Gk soloikismos f. soloikos speaking incorrectly*]). Even its use of brackets must be correct. I need to choose my words with the felicity associated with learned writing. On the other hand, this is a chapter offering a sustained, even angry, critique of the haughtiness that goes with secure membership of the academy; so ought I not to write roughly, in a style down-to-earth, unmannerly? I don't have the nerve to do that, or the confidence that the force of the argument will win against the disdainful reception of such a crude manner of expression. What shall I do? The answer, typically postmodern, is that of the self-conscious flâneur, posturing as what he really is, so as to escape the shame of being detected in full frontal self-disclosure. *We are arrant knaves, all; believe none of us* is Hamlet's advice to Ophelia (III.i.128), condescending to what he perceives to be her naïveté, and at the same time enjoying his own evident sophistication. But there is a sincerity there, too; even anguish. The predicament of this chapter derives from my willing complicity in the maintaining of an academic élite, which I disapprove of but to which I want to be seen to belong. It is a predicament which may be shared by both writer and readers. We need a way out of this dilemma, so that writers and readers are at ease with, and mutually respectful of, a range of manners of speaking, erudite or down-to-earth, couth or uncouth.

I began with a reference to Conrad's *Heart of Darkness*, a tale about a mission to rescue a representative of the civilised world from the heart of the African jungle in which he appears mysteriously to have made his home. The nightmare vision offered to the *fin de siècle* reader is that Mr Kurtz may have 'gone native', gone over to the other side, losing that sense of himself as missionary, sent from a place of light to a place of darkness, becoming 'black', in all the menacing senses of that word for a late Victorian reader. What this civilised person has encountered in the heart of darkness, is 'horror'. The story cannot tell us what that is for there are no words to describe it. Language fails in the encounter with what the narrator calls the *supreme moment of complete knowledge*: a knowledge which is more than words can say. The project of the narrator, to bring Mr Kurtz home, fails of necessity, since Mr Kurtz cannot be saved. Like Faustus, he knows too much to be brought back within the pale of the ideas and values of what the novel uneasily recognises as a cramped correctness. Crucially, *Heart of Darkness* cannot say what Mr Kurtz knows because the novel itself belongs to, and is an example of, the discourse of late Victorian English high culture; the encounter it wants to understand is between that discourse and the Other, a way of thinking and experiencing which cannot be expressed in English prose. The written English words can tell us only what that alien knowledge is not: it is not educated, not civilised, not Christian. What makes the novel shudder is inexpressible darkness – the recognition that there is that which our discourse cannot know or say, a darkness in which the educated are lost for words.

It is a grotesque insult, but one which this chapter has argued is encoded in educational discourse, to imagine the predicament of adult learners in a comparable way: to position them as helpless and in need of rescue. A more balanced view of education is suggested in the sub-title of this chapter, the line from the poem by Robert Frost. The full text of the poem is:

Revelation

We make ourselves a place apart
Behind light words that tease and flout,
But oh, the agitated heart
Till someone really find us out.

'Tis pity if the case require
(Or so we say) that in the end
We speak the literal to inspire
The understanding of a friend.

But so with all, from babes that play
At hide-and-seek to God afar,
So all who hide too far away
Must speak and tell us where they are.

Inspiring the understanding of a friend is a helpful way of imagining the encounter between teacher and learner in post-compulsory education, but only if the understanding is held to move both ways. It challenges the positioning of educators as superior, expecting to disdain, and of learners as their inferiors, expecting to be disdained. The 'literal' which needs to be spoken is the telling one-another 'where [we] are', a disclosure that strips away the pretences and pretensions of the educators, ending the masquerade, and at the same time enables the plain speaking of the learners as they speak their minds. Educators then become learners and learners educators (McNiff 1993: 217). In legal parlance this is called 'full disclosure': each side knows everything; or perhaps we should say that between the parties, educators and learners, there has been a full exchange of words. The deal between teachers and learners needs to recognise the strangeness of each other's words: that the process of making them our own is one of making accommodations between our own and each other's wordplay. Education then becomes conference, discourse: the mingling of friends' words which brings about exchanges, comparisons and contrasts, and which leads to comprehension, literally, 'grasping together'.

This brings me to Levinas, whose philosophy urges us to take each other seriously; indeed, he wants the Other to be written with a capital letter, to signify that there is something more about another person that just their being 'not-me'. There is a strangeness about strangers which he more than respects; it seems to him to disclose that alterity towards which metaphysical desire tends: 'something else entirely . . . the absolutely other' (Levinas 1998: 77). This is the language of religious mysticism; but Levinas insists (*ibid*: 77) that atheism is the prerequisite of the kind of encounter he seeks.

Levinas' ideas are dense, strange and beautiful. Levinas (*ibid*: 45) writes:

> To affirm the priority of *Being* over *existents* is to already decide the essence of philosophy; it is to subordinate the relation with *someone*, who is an existent, (the ethical relation) to a relation with the *Being of existents*, which, impersonal, permits the apprehension, the domination of existents (a relationship of knowing), subordinates justice to freedom.

What is swept away here, in the characteristic gesture of phenomenology, is the primacy of being: that way of knowing which privileges essence – the knowing what a person is – over the encounter, the meeting, the grasping together of comprehension. For Levinas, this reconciliation is brought about through language, the mingling discussed above. Levinas writes (*ibid*: 67):

> One can, to be sure, conceive of language as an act, as a gesture of behaviour. But then one omits the essential of language: the coinciding of the revealer and the revealed in the face, which is

114

accomplished in being situated in height with respect to us – in teaching. And, conversely, gestures and acts produced can become, like words, a revelation, that is . . . a teaching.

'The coinciding of the revealer and the revealed in the face' makes language, and, by extension, teaching, an act of recognition: teacher and learner (and their roles are reciprocal) 'being situated in height with respect to us', recognise face-to-face their otherness-togetherness. They like, and are like, each other: learning is liking.[10]

Levinas is here adopting a position which is the polar opposite of that of Berkeley, whose *esse est percipi*[11] makes being perceived the condition for existence of inanimate objects. By contrast, Levinas holds that my being *derives* from my knowing the Other: I am, not because I am perceived but because there is an Other whom I perceive, in the knowing of whom I am sustained in being. He writes (*ibid*: 88):

> To posit knowing as the very existing of the creature, as a tracing back beyond the condition to the other that founds, is to separate oneself from a whole philosophical tradition that sought the foundation of the self in the self, outside of heteronomous opinions. We think that existence for itself is not the ultimate meaning of knowing, but rather the putting back into question of the self, the turning back to what is prior to oneself, in the presence of the Other.

Levinas is telling us, in his elliptical way, that what matters is other people.[12] Studying something (such as the being of another person) misses the point, the presence before our gaze of that other person, who is known not by study but by encounter. Because what matters is people, ethics takes priority over ontology – we consider primarily what we should do rather than what may or may not be. Teaching, then, becomes 'the coinciding of the revealer and the revealed in the face', a 'revealed' who, as he awkwardly puts it, is *in height with respect to us*, that is to say, on a par, our equal. This encounter makes me what I am. I am what I am by virtue of my being confronted by the Other.

This chapter began with a parade of learning intended to pique, intrigue, frustrate and at the same time impress the reader. The point was to reproduce the experience of students entering the academy, learning as best they can to negotiate admission to its strange and intimidating discourse. Ending the chapter with Levinas confronts us with mysterious discourse of another kind, for Levinas is not parading his learning or disparaging ours. His project is to engage us in a friendship of strangers, who come alive in encountering each other. Language cannot replicate, still less replace, that encounter, which is why the writing baffles us with its hints and suggestions, its mystical strangeness, defeating the expectations of the learned reader, whose true learning only begins in the strange presence of the Other. What are we talking about? Levinas offers no answer to that reasonable question. 'Questioning' says Levinas (*ibid*: 96) 'is not explained by astonishment only, but by the presence of him to whom it is addressed.'

Notes

1. Plato is consistently scathing about the sophists, amongst other things for their mindless regurgitation of public opinion (he regards the public as 'the great beast') (*Republic* 196); but the key text is the *Phaedrus*. For a discussion of Nietzsche's defence of sophistry see Norris 1991, pp60–64.
2. The article reminds us that Eliot toyed with the idea of using 'The horror! The horror!' as an epigraph for *The Waste Land*. The epigraph for *The Hollow Men* is another climacteric line from *Heart of Darkness*: 'Mistah Kurtz – he dead.'
3. Google is a search engine
4. This is not to argue that using words like 'Phenomenology' is useless, any more than using a word like 'Scandinavia' is useless. At least we know (following Saussure – the key text here is the *General Course in Linguistics*: 120ff) when someone says 'Scandinavia', that they do not mean us to think about Africa, Asia, America, etc. We know what they do *not* mean.
5. Certificate in Education and Post-Graduate Certificate in Education, Post-Compulsory Education and Training. These are courses which offer serving teachers in the Post-Compulsory sector, (Further and Higher Education, Adult and Continuing Education, etc.) together with recent graduates wishing to teach in this sector, the qualifications they need.
6. John Stuart Mill, in 'What is Poetry?' (1833, revised 1859): 'Poetry and eloquence are both alike the expression or utterance of feeling; but, if we may be excused the antithesis, we should say that eloquence is *heard*; poetry is *over*heard. Eloquence supposes an audience. The peculiarity of poetry appears to us to lie in the poet's utter unconsciousness of a listener.'
7. I Corinthians XIV 1–19. Paul is faced with a dilemma here. He recognises the privileged status of transcendent utterance of this kind, associated as it is, in the minds of the believers, with divine inspiration; but the sober educator in him is impatient with what is, in effect, a private communication between the ecstatic and God, to which, as he dryly remarks, *he that occupieth the room of the unlearned [cannot] say Amen . . . seeing he understandeth not what thou sayest* . . . (And in quoting from the King James version I am myself employing something akin to glossalalia, wrapping my reference in the eloquence of four centuries past so as to accord it (confer on it?) a dignity and status above the level of common (vulgar) speech.

8. A small minority of those responding *wanted* the language to be difficult:

   Oversimplifying language in lectures is a bit too like dumbing down: we want to get to the higher level, not to be talked down to from above. There needs to be a sense of strangeness about new learning; otherwise there's no challenge.

9. Literally 'a teaching of secret things'. The 'disciplina arcani' is described in *The Oxford Dictionary of the Christian Church* as 'The practice ascribed to the early Church of concealing certain theological doctrines and religious usages from catechumens and pagans.'

10. These ideas recall another, and later, poem of Frost's, which this time he calls *All Revelation* (1971: .332)

    Eyes seeking the response of eyes
    bring out the stars, bring out the flowers,
    Thus concentrating earth and skies
    So none need be afraid of size.
    All revelation has been ours.

11. 'To be is to be perceived.' Berkeley, in his *Treatise Concerning the Principles of Human Knowledge* (1710), asserts (para. 3) of 'unthinking things' that 'their esse is percipi, nor is it possible they should have any existence, out of the minds of thinking things which perceive them' – on the ground that unthinking things, 'sensible objects', are 'ideas or sensations'. (http: //www.xrefer.com/entry/551953)

12. Compare the comment of Jean Paul Sartre (from his 1947 play *No Exit*, recalled on his death 15 Apr 80): *Hell is other people.*

9

'I've made it more academic, by adding some snob words from the thesaurus'

ELIZABETH BURN and TERRY FINNIGAN

This chapter uses plain speaking to tell plain truths: like Satterthwaite, Elizabeth Burn and Terry Finnigan draw on participants' voices to explore the notion of being an outsider in the academy, and to challenge the mystification of learning which the academy maintains through its use of language. Like the FE lecturers described by Harrison, Burn and Finnigan's research participants are engaged in difficult games of boundary-crossing; and like the non-western learners described in Nichols' chapter, they find that crossing the boundary still does not necessarily win them academic recognition.

Introduction

Do students at university construct themselves as academic or non-academic, and does this learning identity influence their subsequent achievements? This was the question we were recently debating as two female tutors who teach in an inner city university that has a mission to recruit non-traditional students[1] into Higher Education. The discussion arose out of our increasing concern that many of the students we teach seem to doubt their potential either to contribute verbally in classroom discussions and presentations, or to write academic assignments. The outcome of this reflection on our individual teaching contacts with our students has led to the shared writing of this chapter. Sharing student voices that we listen to both in tutorials and teaching sessions helps us to understand that the ongoing self-identification by some students as non-academic, despite achieving entry into university, is perhaps a normal response to an institutional culture that Bhopal (1994: 130) describes in the following way:

> The language of academia is white, middle-class and male. There exists a hierarchy within academia, one which has boundaries whose membership are defined by white middle-class academics.

The student body that we teach is predominately female and from a diverse range of ethnicities. A considerable number are multilingual and many are mature students from economically disadvantaged backgrounds. A substantial number of our students represent groups in society that have been and still are disadvantaged in terms of educational access, although, as Leonard points out, there have been significant moves towards widening participation:

> During the past two decades, universities have attempted to widen access by encouraging the participation of previously under-represented groups such as women, members of the working-class and minority ethnic groups.
>
> (Leonard 1994: 163)

However, in Plummer's view, this has had little effect:

> Social class forms the basis for differentiation, segregation and failure in education. The education system continues to favour the already privileged . . .
>
> (Plummer 2000: 43)

Plummer points out (2000: 38) that while 80 per cent of high-income teenagers currently go to university, 86 per cent of teenagers from low-income groups do not, while Reay (1998: 165) argues that acknowledging class bias has 'become increasingly problematic within a contemporary educational marketplace underpinned by a rhetoric of classlessness.' Denial of this institutional discrimination pathologises the individual working-class student, rather than the education system, as the problem, and perpetuates class-based differences in academic achievement. This pattern is reflected in Walkerdine, Lucey and Melody's recent study (2001) of working-class and middle-class girls growing up in today's educational market place, which found continuing evidence of a huge class divide in attainment in Britain.

This chapter is in three parts. In part one, we introduce ourselves, reflecting on how we experience our own academic position within the university. Part two is dedicated to student voices, where we give examples of students' constructions of themselves as learners within higher education. The concluding section outlines four areas within higher education in which strategies can be developed to support more fair and equitable practices.

Part One: Lecturers' Voices

Terry

I come from a white working-class background and I was the first member of my extended family to go to University. I worked for over sixteen years in the Further Education Sector in inner London with a range of non-traditional students such as mature adults and young refugees, whose ultimate ambition was to study at University. I gained my MA through part time evening study as I was bringing up my two children and working two days a week. Therefore, I myself also came from a non-traditional background into the Academy.

I have now been working for three years as a part time lecturer in English for Academic Purposes in a university faculty of Humanities and Education faculty. The students who attend my classes are drawn from across the university, and either opt to attend by their own choice or are recommended to attend by university tutors. I often still feel that I myself do not belong here and I identify with the students I teach. Many of these students have arrived at University through access routes[2] and initially feel very under confident about their academic skills.

During the sessions students often share their fears and concerns, such as feeling unclear about what academic writing should look like. In group discussions I encourage students to reflect on the writing strategies they already use and focus on their strengths. I also hold numerous individual tutorials with students when they are working on their first essay, to discuss their ideas and the language they use to express them. Sometimes the fear of writing is so great that they suffer mental blocks which cause them to delay the writing until the last minute, so the essay that is given in is really the first draft. When the essays have been marked we have sessions reflecting on the comments made by tutors and discussing ways to develop other work.

Academic writing is not the only work that is covered with the students. As many of them have to complete school experience placements, we also discuss the difference between spoken Standard English and other language varieties within the classroom. They often meet some resistance to their accent and dialect, and their subsequent reflections make them feel like outsiders who do not fit in with the other staff.

My position as a language support tutor is in itself a marginalized one within the overall organisation, and this is aggravated by my part time status. However, the space it provides for the students is powerful in terms of reflecting on practices and discussing fears in a non-threatening environment.

Elizabeth

I am a white working-class woman who has taught in the university for eleven years as a senior lecturer in education after a long period of primary school teaching. I have combined my teaching with raising a family of three children and continuing academic study. My own non-traditional background, with a first degree and MA gained through part-time study with the Open University, allows me to feel empathy with many of our students. The fact that I have attempted to retain my working-class accent and culture positions me differently from my middle-class colleagues. This is similar to the experience of Wise (1997) who found that when she became a university lecturer, after being a social work practitioner who had gained a PhD, her class background meant that both students and middle-class colleagues questioned her academic ability:

> At the same time that they turn to me as an 'authority', the students simultaneously deny that authority by virtue of the fact that I am too much 'like them'. I am too nice to be taken seriously as an academic . . . Perhaps most important of all, if I don't dress things up in mystificatory language and am able to explain complex phenomena in everyday accessible language, then I do not pass the 'real academic' test.
>
> (Wise 1997: 127)

Like Wise, I find many areas of commonality with our working-class students and I now actively employ this as a feature of my practice. I also find my class position brings both advantages and disadvantages within the academy. In my personal tutorials, students say they can talk to me and I sense that this is linked to both my age and gender as well as to my working-class accent. Does my female working-class physicality and accent, that so marks me as Other (Burn 2000: 59) in academic circles, make me accessible to students who themselves are alien in the university culture? Hey describes how she uses her northern vernacular in the academy, often to tactical advantage, since in interviews her accent 'elicits and offers sympathy' (1997: 146). Skeggs, on the other hand, describes the way in which her identity was delegitimated when she entered university as a mature white working-class woman. 'I had been recognised,' she writes, 'as common, authentic and without much cultural value' (1997a: 130). hooks experienced the same deligitimation, and reflects in her writing (2000: 28) on the 'class shame' she felt when starting college. Many of the mature students I listen to express similar feelings of class alienation. hooks outlines the consequences that students who attempt to maintain their own culture can face:

> Students who enter the academy unwilling to accept without question the assumptions and values held by privileged classes tend to be silenced, deemed troublemakers.
>
> (hooks 1994: 179)

My own position as a lecturer in early years mathematics in a School of Education mainly concerned with teacher education contributes to my institutional placing as not a real academic due to the traditional university hierarchies of power. The discipline of education is given less 'intellectual confidence' (Evans 1997: 51) than those of philosophy or the natural sciences. Maguire (1996: 32) found that mature women like myself teaching in higher education were often regarded as 'educationalists not academics'. Maguire discusses how these mature women could be positioned as mothers, while Dillabough (2000: 176) quotes a female teacher educator who argues she is 'not your mother' when male colleagues attempt to define her as such. I am often asked by male colleagues to take on their female personal students as I am seen as having more empathy due to my age and gender. This also serves to release them from the 'emotional work' that can be viewed as non-academic (see Luttrell 1997 for a fuller discussion of the devaluation of the caregiving side of teaching and learning).

Do mature working-class students (female and male) disclose their academic worries to me as an imagined kindly mother or indeed grandmother figure, rather than as an academic? Walsh points out the dangers of engaging in the false dichotomy between emotional conversation and academic conventions. She argues instead for a healing alliance between students and tutors which includes the seemingly insignificant personal and emotional conversations which can be dismissed and indeed derided within university culture:

> The lack of status afforded conversation is, of course, essential to the construction of the academic voice and its separation from ordinary life.
>
> (Walsh 1996: 197)

hooks (1994: 193) likewise challenges this damaging divide between the rational and emotional within higher education. She urges feminist pedagogy to defy the classed, racialised and gendered aspects of the mind/body split, and emphasises the need to legitimate emotionality as part of academic learning, rather than seeing 'emotional outbursts' as 'vulgar disruptions of classroom social order' (1994: 178). Similarly, in her study of ten non-traditional students in higher education, Lillis (2001: 115) laments the fact that logic and academic truth is valued more than emotion and personal experience within the academy. This is reflected in my own research (Burn 2001), where 'it's not for the likes of us' is an on-going theme of many of the interviews I have held with schoolteachers from non-traditional backgrounds after they have qualified from universities.

As well as academic language difference, the cultural traditions of university can result in a belief that only certain students have a right to be there. Leonard found that for mature non-traditional students, the entry into university was traumatic even after completing access courses:

> All the mature students came from working-class backgrounds and felt intimidated by the sophisticated language that seemed to come from academic staff.
>
> (Leonard 1994: 169)

My own status within the university, in common with that of Medhurst (2000), is marked by class contradictions. I now have a middle-class lifestyle yet, like Medhurst, I too do not feel middle-class (2000: 20). My continuing 'ambivalence, subordination and struggle' (Hey 1997: 144) within the university culture places me as a non-traditional tutor, and this allows for a different negotiation in the student/tutor power relationship to occur – one that evidences classed subjectivities, whether I want it to or not. This is clearly reflected in my contribution to this chapter: I am not a neutral observer of the situation I am describing.

Part Two: Student Voices

The title of this chapter was taken from a telephone conversation with Sabia, a mature Bangladeshi woman student who was completing her final year dissertation in order to gain a BA degree in Educational Studies. The student worked in a school as a classroom support assistant and was studying part-time as well as bringing up a family. After several years of university study she had clearly internalised the notion that in order to write academically you needed to 'add some snob words'. The subject of her final Project was her own workplace experience of supporting bilingual children, yet she thought that only the usage of alien words would allow her to gain her degree. This student concentrated on finding academic vocabulary to use in the text rather than developing her thesis. Her phone call was meant to re-assure the tutor ('Don't worry, Elizabeth') that she had learnt the unspoken academic writing rules. This non-traditional student divides language into the academic snob words and the real ones that she, as an articulate bilingual woman, uses in real life.

Jen, a white mature monolingual working-class female BEd student in her final year of study, describes the academic language she uses for writing:

> The type of language I rarely use when speaking to my peers; the type of language that I don't readily understand; and the type of language that means spending hours at a computer turning something quite simple into something that sounds moderately impressive with elitist results.

The spoken voice of non-traditional students (in terms of both accent and dialect) is likewise something to hide or disguise in university classrooms. In a maths session Elizabeth showed a video of her own classroom teaching. Two of the students in the group came to see her afterwards in her room 'for a word in private.' The black African Caribbean woman admitted she had worked hard to lose her Birmingham accent before starting university since she thought it would make her sound stupid. The white working-class woman disclosed that she was very ashamed of her strong Cockney accent. The short video clip, which was meant to support discussion of teacher/ pupil maths dialogue, had shocked the group. It seemed that they couldn't believe that Elizabeth would keep her working-class accent when being interviewed for a national training video. This is despite the fact she had been teaching them for twelve weeks with the same voice! The intense discussion ended with the black student encouraging the white student to speak more in class, as there was 'nothing wrong with speaking Cockney'.

While a Cockney accent may just pass as acceptable in the classroom, Cockney dialect does not. Since this conversation Elizabeth has been approached by a number of students (female, male, bilingual, monolingual, black, white) who during their school experience have been told by a range of adults – from head teachers to university tutors – not to use their Cockney dialect in the classroom as it is teaching the children 'bad grammar'.

After teaching in schools some students return feeling very under confident about their spoken skills, and this issue is addressed in Terry's teaching sessions. One young student with a Cockney accent expressed her concern to Terry:

> They speak a whole different language out there. I started out feeling excited about working with the kids and ended up feeling silenced. No one said anything but I felt different from the other teachers in the school.
>
> A white-working-class female student

Another white-working-class female student was asked to come and see Terry in order to have lessons so that she could change her use of spoken language. Under the guise of improving speech to be grammatically correct there is a clear message being sent to students

126

that non-standard spoken forms are not acceptable. As Milroy puts it:

> In an age when discrimination in terms of race, colour, religion or gender is not publicly acceptable, the last bastion of overt social discrimination will continue to be a person's use of language.
>
> (in Bauer and Trudgill 1998: 65)

The combined effects of these multiple forms of alienation can be seen clearly in students' own constructions of themselves as outsiders within the academic community, as can be seen in the following examples from student evaluations and interviews.

Examples of student evaluations from Terry's language workshops

As an introduction to her sessions, Terry asks students to reflect on their approaches to academic writing:

> My strength is that I can discuss the essay fully. I still have difficulties in writing in an academic style.
>
> A black female working-class Education student

> I normally work on an essay two days before the deadline therefore I am in a terrible panic and I add any sort of information just to make the essay flow and to hand it in.
>
> A white male working-class Education student

When the students have their essays marked Terry discusses with the students how to use the feedback in a constructive way. Some students have found their own solutions to their initial concerns about academic writing and they talk about the importance of working with others during the initial stages of the writing process:

> I work well with a group because seeing others working motivates me as I feel I'm not on my own.
>
> A white female working-class Teaching student

> Being able to be part of a study group helped a lot this time especially when hitting a mental block.

Finally, Terry asks students to reflect on the effect the workshops have had on their experience of academic writing:

> At the beginning of my academic year I had no idea how to write academic English and also what kind of English, I should be writing

because firstly, English is not my first language and secondly because I was out of education for so long time. So I was feeling uncomfortable at the beginning but all that has changed now and at least I understand which way to start.

> A black female working-class Women's Studies student

The most important thing about this session has been time. Terry had time to talk to me and because of the language that I am studying which I find is extremely difficult, and Terry has been able to explain to me and how to focus on the question . . . I feel that I have improved a lot because in Performing Arts there isn't much time for teachers to sit with students about their work. It is good to have someone who has time.

> A black female working-class Performing Arts student

It would seem that the workshops were really helpful . . . returning to academic education after thirty years the skill of writing can be taught and is not some high prize only for the gifted, it is for everyone.

> A white male working-class History student

Comments collected in the course of Elizabeth's ongoing research with non-traditional trainee and qualified teachers

These comments reflect the continuing lack of confidence experienced by students and teachers:

> I'm not academic by nature.
>
> > A white female working-class Early Years student

> They belong there more than I do . . . it belongs to them . . . I felt: 'Oh God it's a University' . . . I'm sorry . . . but I'm just like . . . an outsider . . .
>
> > A black female working-class student teacher

> . . . theories . . . they'd all be coming from white middle-class perspectives . . . it never made sense to me . . .
>
> > A black male working-class student teacher

> I think because I am a white working-class female . . . even having an MA is sort of . . . quite detrimental anyway . . . but having an MA . . . coming from a working-class background, working in a school and being . . . successful and young . . . is not liked . . . and wanting to do a PhD and always reading . . . people just don't like it.
>
> > A white female working-class Early Years teacher

I still couldn't quite believe it you know . . . that they wanted me. That I was good enough you know . . . when I got there I kept thinking: 'they are going to find out and chuck me out . . .

A white female working-class primary teacher

. . . this place is not for the likes of us . . . they don't really like working-class people . . .

A white female working-class student teacher

We suggest that these and similar examples of students' comments could be used to open up dialogue about the continuing elitism within universities and society. All of the students and teachers referred to have succeeded academically and have given their permission to be quoted in the hope that their voices can help challenge present exclusionary practices.

The cumulative results of spoken and written difference, alongside an increasingly standardised curriculum content in higher education and the endorsement of white middle-class cultural behaviours is difficult to imagine if you have not experienced it from a working-class standpoint. It is in student voices that the complex institutional nature of continuing bias against non-traditional students can perhaps be glimpsed. These students' academic achievements well demonstrate their ability to overcome institutional bias. This bias constitutes a sort of institutional illness, for which we have listened to many of the symptoms; but the illness is to be found in the institutions, not in the students. The terms 'non-traditional' and 'poor' have themselves attracted a mythology of educational stigma (see Tomlinson 2000 for a clear analysis of the continuation of this public propaganda), again perpetuating the idea that the students constitute the problem. Students have spoken to us about negative labels being applied to our university due to the fact that we recruit a high number of non-traditional students compared to more traditional universities. Ainley (1994: 65) discusses how non-traditional students can 'pick up their perception of their place at the bottom of the hierarchy:' a perception which reinforces their identities as non-academic, whatever their achievements.

Conclusions

In this section, we make recommedations in four areas, arising from the experiences discussed in this chapter. Firstly, we argue for opportunities for students to develop a critical consciousness as part of their university experience; secondly, we argue for a change in teaching practices to recognise the oral as well as the written; thirdly, we discuss the production of shared stories as a political act; and finally, we discuss issues related to staffing, recruitment and professional development within the university.

1. Critical consciousness: reading and writing the world

Sabia, whose words titled this chapter, needs the opportunity, with other university students, to review research that shows how 'the failure of black students is not their responsibility, but that of the policies discriminating against them' (Freire 1996: 176).

The 'banking system' of education, as Freire described it, by which knowledge is depositied within a passive student body, must be replaced by education for critical consciousness that develops awareness of how educational processes operate to silence subordinate voices (Giroux 1992: 14). This is particularly urgent within initial teacher education, where opportunities for students as 'critical co-investigators' (Freire 1970: 62) to carry out wider reflection on learning cultures are increasingly limited by a narrow skills based Standards curriculum, imposed by the State and regularly inspected by Ofsted[3] (Cole 1999a). Fielding (2001: 108) identifies the 'intellectual poverty' of this discourse of delivery with 'the clutter of criteria and the tyranny of targets' that pervades present UK education policymaking and practice.

Students as well as staff need to be invited to 'politicise the process of education' (Giroux 1992: 16). hooks (1994: 189) discusses the need to develop an engaged pedagogy in university teaching: a pedagogy that recognises the importance of confronting issues of class alongside race and gender discriminations; while Thompson (2000: 178) warns us that 'theoretical discussions about diversity and power are in danger of becoming ossified.' Students need the opportunity to undertake critical study of the writings of Freire, hooks, Giroux and others who challenge the present practices of so-called neutral education.

These writers represent diverse social groups and speak from their own teaching experience within the traditional academy: an academy that is itself still constituted on maintaining present hierarchies that exclude the Other.

Rather than viewing the students as the problem, assumptions about what is defined as *rational, neutral* knowledge in the academy need to be problematised, and students' own lived experiences and languages must become part of the learning curriculum instead of being excluded by it. Academic terminology needs to be deconstructed rather than used to maintain the status quo, and students as well as staff should be involved in this process. Language is central to the maintenance of power inequalities: none of us stand outside the class, race and gender hierarchies that we study (Skeggs 1997b).

2. Teaching Pracitices: challenging the oral/written divide

The opportunity to talk about the process of academic writing rather than view it as a talent that some students naturally have and other students have not is vital. Freire (1996: 171) highlights the importance of this:

> The oral moment must precede the writing moment, which we also need to talk about as much as possible. Talking about what one intends to write and what one has already written about helps one to better write what one has not written and rewrite what has not been finished.

When students (and tutors) discuss their own writing journeys it validates the production of an academic document as more than a trawl through a thesaurus in order to pass as academic, and avoids the danger of mistaking dense words for thought. It also serves to legitimate students' own language and invites critical reflection from a variety of perspectives. This does not deny the centrality of intellectual discipline, but recognises Freire's view of what academia should be:

> Academia cannot and must not become an inhibiting context that limits the ability to think, argue, inquire, doubt or go beyond existing models.
>
> (Freire 1996b: 169)

To make this a possibility, all students must feel that their voices are heard and recognised within the academy:

Questions about who is allowed to speak remind us that encounters are always framed by the realities of power and that these matters are invariably significant, especially to those who seem to have less of it . . .To talk about student voice is misleading. Some voices (middle-class girls) seem more willing to speak than others . . .

(Fielding 2001: 101)

After a teaching session concerned with equal access issues and mathematics, a mature white working-class student stayed behind to ask Elizabeth if she had talked too much or sounded stupid. How do tutors enable all students to have both the right and responsibility to contribute to class discussions? How do teachers in university settings promote the 'constructive dialogue' that hooks (1994: 179) advocates?

3. Producing shared stories as a political act

This chapter arose out of both the listening to and telling of learning stories. As Thompson (2000: 6) points out in relation to her exploration of women, class and educational access,'personal narratives provide the starting point at least' for an understanding of the factors which alienate non-traditional students in academia. However, she recognises the dangers of self-indulgence and emphasises that 'it is what becomes of the stories that matters' (*ibid:* 7). By taking 'storied selves' (Luttrell 1997: 118) as a starting point, we can gain a deeper understanding of the 'institutional practices and policies that acknowledge and validate certain types of students at the expense of others' (*ibid:* 122). Stories told or written make visible the emotional aspects of the learning process that Luttrell sees as a 'taboo subject amongst most educators' (*ibid:* 122).

Tett (2000) suggests that we view students' recollected accounts as making sense, both symbolically and narratively, of a range of possibilities. These recollected accounts can beome teaching and research materials in their own right, as we have found in work with our own students. For example, a dyslexic student's account of her learning journey (written alongside Elizabeth and her tutor) has been published in a dyslexia journal (Morgan and Burn 2000); a video of twelve non-traditional students telling their stories was the focus of a conference paper written by Elizabeth and published on the ERIC database 2000 (Listening to Students); and an account of a mature woman's mathematics journey was published as a joint text with Elizabeth's summary of relevant research in the field (Walker 1999; Burn 1999). These texts and the video have subsequently been used by colleagues in teaching sessions.

These strategies, as well as valuing students' oral and written educational stories, can provide new teaching materials for opening up critical dialogue in university classrooms and critical reflection on learning cultures, exploring Plummer's view (2000) that academic texts are always middle-class. In a retelling of Open University students' educational journeys, Lunneborg (1994: 51) shares the story of Judy Giles who, even after achieving a doctorate, feels that she doesn't belong:

> She sometimes irrationally feels that the academic skills she has gained might be taken away and that working-class folks like her can never be part of the middle-class intellectual community.

These shared stories, supported by theory and research, form a powerful agent for change in the academy.

4. *Staffing the university: recruitment and continuing professional development*

The *illness* that we identified earlier in the chapter, and that continues to infect the university, is evidenced in staffing patterns that re-affirm traditional discriminations. More tutors who represent groups that have been marginalised need recruiting into higher education. There needs to be a recruitment policy that aims to appoint tutors that represent our society, challenging elitist staffing and biased promotion patterns (Dillabough 2000). In addition, all higher education staff need to be aware, through regular opportunities for continuing professional development, of which groups of students are under-achieving and under-represented, and of the policy/practice implications of this under-achievement. We need opportunities to reflect on our teaching, while student/staff research seminars (Brice Heath 1991: 13) could allow us all to become 'jointly active in the learning process'.

We realise that these suggestions have resourcing implications and that in the present economic circumstances many universities are unable or unwilling to fund new developments, but education as the practice of freedom (hooks 1994) does not necessarily depend on economics. As she puts it:

> The academy is not paradise. But learning is a place where paradise can be created. The classroom, with all its limitations, remains a location of possibility.
>
> (hooks 1994: 207)

Notes

1. Whilst employing the term 'non-traditional students' throughout this chapter, we wish to make it clear that in no way are we using this label in an insulting way, but we are using it as a reminder that these are the students who are still being disadvantaged in an elitist educational culture.

2. While entry into English universities has traditionally been by means of gaining A-Level (Advanced Level) qualifications, usually taken by eighteen-year-olds in their final year of school, widening participation policies over the last decade or so have led to an increased recruitment of students who do not hold these qualifications, but have taken one of a range of specific courses, broadly described as access courses, aimed at preparing both young and mature learners for university study.

3. Ofsted (the Office for Standards in Education) is the inspecting body for schools and initial teacher training in England.

10

'They just won't critique anything': The 'problem' of international students in the Western academy

SUSAN NICHOLS

Susan Nichols echoes the discourse analysis employed by Colley and Hursh, offering a deconstruction of the discourses of identity which create non-Western learners as Other. Set in the context of Australian Higher Education, the chapter explores issues of identity through a critique of the rhetoric of the global education market and the discourses of business and media. Like Burn and Finnigan, Nichols is concerned about who is excluded from the academy, and for what reasons; and like Quinn and Colley, she suggests that the refusal to participate, on the part of the outsider, constitutes a form of resistance in its own right.

Narrative 1

A doctoral student in the early stages of her program, Ji-Ching came away from a meeting with her supervisor feeling depressed. She had just been challenged to develop her own perspective on the research topic. But the problem was that everything she read sounded so convincing, so skilfully argued. She did not know enough about her topic yet to judge what would be the best perspective to take. Some days she wondered whether she would ever have anything original to contribute.

Narrative 2

'They just won't critique anything.' The exasperated lecturer was speaking about a small group of South-East Asian students within her Masters program at an Australian university. She had tried explaining to them, she said, that a critical approach to the literature was necessary at this level. 'They just accept everything they read. They're just too polite to question it.' How, she wondered, were they ever going to write their literature reviews?

These two anecdotes illustrate the difficulty that international students have with the practice of scholarly critique within Western universities. This is not surprising since they come from cultures where independent thinking is not valued as highly as other qualities such as respect for authority. It is not surprising that Ji-Ching struggled with finding her own perspective on her research topic and was so readily persuaded by the arguments of experts.

Except that Ji-Ching was not her real name. It was Susan. She was not an international student. Her struggles could not be attributed to cultural origin and nobody called her passive or dependent. Because of this her supervisors continued to ask the hard questions, confident that she would eventually develop a critical stance. She continued to accept what she read until she had developed a map of the theoretical terrain and could begin to navigate herself around it. Eventually she successfully completed her doctorate, got a job in the academy and began writing articles for publication. In fact, she wrote this chapter.

Critique has become a dividing practice in the internationalised university. It functions as a marker of difference, rendering some cultural groups apparently deficient and at the same time establishing a market for the expertise presumably needed to remedy their deficiency. My struggle to construct a critical position was understood as an individual issue, part of my development as a scholar. Other students' struggles are seen as originating with their cultures, thus casting into question their ability or motivation to develop into scholars.

The argument presented here is written from an Australian perspective and so will have different alignments and dissonances with other local contexts. It sets out to build a broad socio-semantic context (Fairclough 1992) within which specific local instances and practices can be interpreted (instances like, for example, the lecturer's complaint above or a newspaper article about plagiarism). This approach involves surveying the field of discourse around a particular subject by assembling and analysing a diverse range of texts. The subject in

136

this case is international students' 'problem' with critique, and the texts have been sourced eclectically from the print media, institutional publications, research journals, historical studies, government press releases and anecdotes. This level of analysis does not involve systematic analysis of particular texts but is rather aimed at producing a reading of the overall context within which meanings are constructed and texts are produced. I begin building this context with a discussion of Australia's position in the global market-place of higher education.

International students in the global marketplace

Consistent with a world-wide trend in education industries, Australian universities have been working hard to position themselves as competitive players in a global marketplace. Australia's shift towards marketisation of the higher education sector has been described as 'unique and unprecedented . . . in the suddenness, the scope [and] the degree of reversal of previous policy' (De Angelis 1998: 98). Over the last five years there has been a dramatic and continuing increase in the proportion of international students within the total enrolment in Australian universities.

The majority of international students in Australian universities come from the South-East Asian region; in particular Malaysia and Singapore. This means that 'international' can often be taken to mean Asian, where 'Asian' is an umbrella term covering a range of non-white, non-Europeans mainly from regions closest geographically to Australia. 'Asian' is a highly contested and inflammatory term in Australian social discourse, therefore it is often avoided in higher education in favour of the more neutral and inclusive term 'international'. I will not be avoiding this term, though, for the very reason that struggles around the meaning of 'Asian' form part of the discursive terrain within which the 'problem' of critique is produced as a subject. Australia's complex relationship with the Asian region is an important factor in understanding the position of international students within the Australian higher education system.

A useful concept for understanding Australia's position within this relationship is that of liminality – a condition of irreconcilable contradiction that arises from the attempt to make a transition from one state to another (Higgot and Nossal 1997). It is argued that

137

Australia's liminal position in relation to Asia is a result of competing forces which drive a return to its Anglo heritage on the one hand and an engagement with the Asian region on the other. Both these drives are realised in policies and practices that produce a range of possible relationships between Australia and Asia, and a range of meanings for the terms 'Australian' and 'Asian'.

It should not be surprising therefore that the subject position of the Asian student in the Australian higher education system should reflect these tensions and contradictions. Globalisation of the higher education sector in Australia has exacerbated this contradictory positioning. On the one hand, international students are seen as 'saviours' of the higher education system. The income they generate has become critical to the financial viability of the Australian higher education sector, particularly since government funding has decreased significantly in the past ten years (Alexander and Rivzi 1993). Educating Australia's neighbours is also seen as advantageous to its interests. While this has long been part of Australia's strategy of maximising its influence, economic globalisation and the deregulation of previously protected markets has intensified the need to build and maintain relationships with current and potential trading partners. International students are often spoken of as ambassadors for Australia and for the Australian universities where they completed their studies. These universities naturally hope that their ambassadors will attract further enrolments.

International students are also seen as contributing directly to Australia's competitiveness by providing a supply of skilled workers. The Federal Government has recently announced changes to its migration policy, easing the way for permanent residence for international students. Hailing this decision, one university claimed that international students could 'plug Australia's brain drain' (Nardelli 2001).

In contrast to this positive rhetoric is the portrayal of international students as inferior students whose access to Australian higher education is based on their ability to pay and the institutions' parlous financial status. This argument unites nationalists (concerned that local students are being squeezed out) with academic traditionalists (concerned that academic standards are being compromised). An example

138

of this hostility appears in a recent article written by a left-wing commentator well-known in Australian circles. The piece begins with an attack on economic rationalism in general and continues:

> And now all this is happening in universities too – the efficiency experts, the downsizing, the compulsory annual redundancies, the winding up of Ancient Greek or Latin . . . by overpaid soft-spoken corporate thugs who want quick profits, quick results and big fees from the sluggard sons of Asian gangsters prepared to pay in hundreds of thousands for the kind of marks that fairness won't allow.
>
> (Ellis 2001: 42)

A legal discourse around criminality is used here to link fee-paying international students ('sons of gangsters') with the corporate entrepreneurs ('thugs') who purportedly sell them degrees. Compared to this brutal coalition is the endangered civilised world represented here by the reference to classical languages (Greek and Latin). The traditional university with its Western knowledge tradition is set in implied opposition to a corrupt global university with a degraded curriculum. Leaving this dramatic rhetoric aside, I turn to a much kinder discourse within which international students are positioned – the discourse of diversity.

Diversity, accountability and critical thinking

In public discourse 'diversity' is generally associated with multiculturalism, a product of Australia's history as a community of invaders and immigrants, a history it shares with many other countries. 'Diversity' is generally taken to be a good thing. We are always 'celebrating diversity' in Australia. This generally means eating and drinking.

In higher education 'diversity' has different meanings, reflecting institutional issues around enrolment patterns and their implications. In the first period of expansion of the sector, the 1970s, 'diversity' referred primarily to age and educational background with the arrival of mature age and alternative entry students. Currently 'diversity' in higher education is largely code for international students and so has come closer to the multicultural meaning that it has in public discourse. The notions of tolerance and celebration sit strangely with the market oriented discourse in which international students are seen as customers. Customers don't require tolerance; they require service.

The celebration of diversity has become somewhat strained in universities these days by an increased emphasis on accountability, with universities internationally under pressure to demonstrate their effectiveness by guaranteeing specific measurable outcomes (Farnham 1999). This has resulted in the development of competency statements tied in to curriculum and assessment. One of the agreed implications of diversity in higher education is that entrants will not all share the same set of values and experiences. But while students may enter the system with different skills and knowledge, they are now expected to exit the system with the same generic set of competencies. You could call it the 'difference-in-same-out' model.

'Critical thinking' occupies an interesting position in current discussions about diversity. It is discussed both as an outcome of a university education and as an essential pre-requisite for success. References to critical thinking in various guises (e.g. 'analytic skills', 'independent thinking', 'reasoning ability' etc) appear in every version of the graduate outcomes statements currently being adopted by Australian universities. If certain groups of entrants are seen as starting with a deficiency in critical thinking, then it is not surprising that these groups will become a focus for anxiety and remedial action.

One outcome of this tension is an attempt to ensure that new entrants already possess particular cognitive skills and dispositions. In Australia, an International Students Admissions Test has been designed to test prospective students' cognitive abilities as an optional part of universities' admissions procedures. This initiative was reported under the heading 'Test of reasoning abilities to clear up doubts' (*The Australian*, September 27, 2001).

Another approach is to take remedial action. An example of this line of thinking is the Critical Practice Project undertaken at one Australian university (Farrell *et al* 1997). The authors explain that this project was a response to concern about 'students' inability to think and write critically' and they specifically mention 'diversity' as the key factor producing this problem. Particular student groups are identified: 'full fee paying International students, adult entry, and [students with] artistic merit' (p154). So those international students who 'buy their way in' are understood, like others who may avoid conventional entry routes into academia, as deficient in some of the intellectual pre-requisites for academic success. Teaching critical thinking becomes a key strategy in compensating for these presumed deficits.

Critical thinking and the ideal subject

In order to explore further the question of why international students are consistently described as deficient in critical thinking, it is helpful to look at how critical thinking is defined, particularly in texts that deal with this issue. I turn here to some definitions quoted in the Critical Practice Project report (Farrell *et al* 1997). My analysis of these definitions begins with the question: What kinds of ideal subjects do these definitions assume? What modes of participation in higher education do these definitions recognise? Conversely, what subjects and modes of participation are rendered invisible or deficient? These questions are important in considering how critical thinking ability in higher education can be identified, taught, learned and assessed.

The first definition states: 'Critical thinking is reasonable reflective thinking that is focused on deciding what to believe and do' (Hagar and Kaye 1992). The key words here are 'reasonable', 'focused' and 'deciding'. Critical thought is rational; it is purposive; and it results in decisions about belief. While these authors are careful to focus on the practice of thinking rather than the subject of the thinker, definitions such as this one can be taken up in ways that produce particular kinds of subjects. The terms in which critical thinking is defined support the notion of an ideal critical thinking subject. At the same time, they imply a problematic non-critical other. If we take the reverse of the terms in this definition, we can construct a definition of this other; one that is irrational, unreflective, unfocussed and indecisive. If we recall that the inability to think critically is seen as a marker of cultural difference, such definitions position the cultural Other as such an irrational subject, consistent with colonialist strategies of representation (Plumwood 1993).

Definitions of critical thinking do more than describe a mode of

141

cognition; they also construct a context within which a particular mode of thinking is enabled, appropriate and expected. The definition just quoted is typical in this respect. It presumes a context in which the subject is free to 'decide what to believe and do'. If critical thinking is Western thinking, then a society which produces the conditions which enable subjects to exercise free agency in their beliefs and actions is, by implication, a Western society. The same deconstructive move that allows us to read the Other non-ideal subject also allows us to read the Other society implied in this definition. This Other society is one where freedom of belief and action is not encouraged. If the non-critical subject is also a non-Western subject, then this implies a non-Western society which produces such a subject.

A comment by a western academic visiting a Chinese university illustrates how social subjects and social contexts are mutually defining in discourse: 'in order for senior theses to be really good, China would have to be a different kind of society, one in which free classroom discussion and independent thinking were encouraged' (Jochnowitz 1986 cited in Pennycook 1998: 185). This statement clearly draws a connection between academic production, social subjectivity and cultural values; authoritarian societies produce dependent thinkers who produce substandard academic work. By characterising cultural others as dependent and uncritical, those of us who are western academics reassure ourselves that we are free, rational individuals.

The second definition reminds us that critical thinking can only be made visible through communicative practices. In academic contexts, the production of written and oral texts is the means by which judgements are made about a student's critical thinking ability. This definition emphasises communication and textual production as means of engaging in critique:

> Analytic habits of thinking, reading, writing, speaking, or discussing . . . [that] go beneath surface impressions, traditional myths, mere opinions, and routine clichés.
>
> (Shor 1993 in Lankshear 1994)

This definition groups textual practices into two categories: analytical practices and others which might be summarised as folk practices. These are not separate but connected through a metaphor of excavation: analytical practices 'go beneath' folk practices in order to unearth something more valuable. Shor's list of surface habits ('impressions, traditional myths, mere opinions, and routine cliches') has much in common with a list of 'cultural resources which have yet to be modernised' which includes 'cultural memories, symbols, myths and sentiment surrounding the ethnic core' (Featherstone 1996: 56). This similarity allows us to see how critical thinking can be located within a modernist discourse of progress. The inclusion of traditional myths in the catalogue of uncritical surface habits reinforces the cultural dimension of this discourse.

When read alongside descriptions of student groups who are presumably deficient in critical thinking skills, such definitions locate the other in the realm of the surface as opposed to the deep realm of rational analysis, and in the domain of traditional practice as opposed to modernist progression. Those holding traditional knowledge (which is given the same status as 'mere opinion') must, presumably, be willing to have this knowledge undermined by rational analysis, and moreover, to participate in this undermining if they are to be considered full members of the academy.

Culture, learning styles and critical thinking

The notion of 'cultural learning style' is one of the means by which the relationship between diversity and educational achievement is explained. This concept combines the idea of learning styles with the idea of cultural difference. In the field of higher education, learning style has most commonly been associated with the broad categories of 'deep' and 'surface' learning which originated with the work of Marton and others in the 1980s (Marton, Hounsell and Entwhistle 1984). Briefly, a learner with a deep approach will seek to transform the knowledge which (s)he encounters, whereas a learner with a surface approach will seek to reproduce it. These two approaches are associated with different practical strategies of processing information.

It can immediately be seen that the surface approach is antithetical to the practice of critique as it is generally understood in the academy. Memorisation is the strategy most strongly associated with a surface approach and this is a key in the positioning of learners from certain cultural backgrounds as uncritical subjects. Rote memorisation is often assumed by westerners to be the prime means of learning in Asian, and particularly Confucian heritage, societies. As Pennycook (1998) points out in his historical overview, this assumption was encouraged by colonial rulers because it reinforced a hierarchy between Western thinkers (portrayed as original, independent and rational) and Eastern thinkers (portrayed as passive and mystical). It also ignored the extent to which rote memorisation was employed as a learning strategy in western educational contexts. Recent research comparing Japanese and Australian students' learning strategies found, contrary to stereotyping, that rote memorisation was preferred more by Western than Eastern heritage students (Purdie, Hattie and Douglas 1996).

Indeed, consistent conclusions about different cultures' attitudes to critical thinking are not easy to find. Research on cultural difference (e.g. Atkinson 1999, Hofstede 1980, Liddicoat 1997, Spizzica 1997, Walker, Bridges and Chan 1996) is widely variable in the ways it defines the term 'culture' (e.g. as value system, country, language); in the methods used to collect and analyse information about culture; and in the resulting descriptions of particular cultures. Cultural differences may be defined as pervasive and enduring patterns of thought (e.g. the 'Western tradition', the 'Confucian tradition'), as interaction practices (e.g. questioning, eye gaze) or as micro-structures within specific written genres (e.g. placement of topic sentences within a research paper). When these typologies are applied to specific questions about learning in higher education contexts, the result is further complexity rather than confirmation of cultural essentialism. If anything, this work reveals the limitations of any single cultural category, making the grouping together of 'international students' on the basis of some assumed common approach to learning an absurdity.

An example of the difficulty of doing this can be found in a study by Meyer and Kiley (1998). The researchers administered a survey to Indonesian postgraduate students in an attempt to investigate whether a cultural approach to learning was responsible for the reported difficulties Indonesian students had with 'the Western approach to *critical thinking*' (authors' italics). The tool for determining learning style was the Meyer Experience of Learning Inventory which uses the familiar deep/surface binary as over-arching categories. Thus the 'Western approach to critical thinking' was associated with a deep approach to learning (and by implication the 'non-Western' with a surface approach).

However, rather than confirming this simple binary, the research revealed new variations, disrupting any attempt to produce an 'Indonesian' learner as opposite to a 'Western' learner. The researchers' response, true to their categorical approach, was to generate new cultural categories – Javanese and non-Javanese. They cautiously concluded that 'some ethnic differences may well be reflected in students' engagement in learning, but in a manner that is not yet amenable to precise interpretation' (1998: 297). That 'not yet', suggests that there are those who hope that, with even more precise learning inventories, academics could manage to categorise every culture and sub-culture, and so fix cultural identities for once and for all.

To complicate matters further, essentialist notions of cultural identity may be employed by national, ethnic and institutional interests in local sites as a means towards furthering their specific agendas. The notion of an 'Asian way' is promoted by some political leaders such as Malaysia's Prime Minister Dr. Mahathir Mohamad (Hamad 2001: *Business Times Malaysia* December 4). This model of cultural identity is formed through the same kind of binary oppositions that are used elsewhere to privilege the Western way. Collectivism and individuality are maintained as opposites, with collectivism more highly valued and individuality portrayed as problematic.

Critical practice in a globalised knowledge market

Far from being restricted to specific cultural contexts, knowledge about critique circulates through the global academic community. Under the conditions of globalisation, scholars do not have to take themselves physically to some specific location in order to encounter the practice of critique. They are able to participate in a global critical community through textual practices such as publishing, electronic discussions and media activities. This allows critiques to be encountered in diverse local sites, to activate multiple agendas and to open up multiple interpretations in a way that challenges any hegemonic discourses. I will now look briefly at how critical practice has been taken up in a site that has been characterised as culturally opposed to so-called Western critical thinking. I refer to China.

Venturino's (2000) discussion of cultural critique in China offers some insight into this complex situation. He describes how economic reforms of the late seventies opened up China to global influences and how resulting demands for globally useful knowledge impacted on higher education curricula and practices. Cultural critique came to be considered a kind of international competence necessary for success-ful participation in the global economy. However this also opened up the floor to subjects previously regarded as subversive – such as the struggles of ethnic minorities. The adoption of 'cultural enquiry' as a legitimate subject in Chinese higher education institutions has pro-vided an opportunity for, amongst others, previously exiled oppo-nents of the Chinese government to find a voice in scholarly debate not only outside China, but within its scholarly community. At the same time, these minority voices are resisted by those in power in the interests of maintaining a Han-centric view of national unity; only certain kinds of cultural critique are granted official status.

A recent paper by sociolinguist Yew-Jin Fang is an example of the global circulation of critique. Fang (2001) advances a critical analysis of Chinese news media discourse in order to demonstrate how report-ing of international events operates to justify Chinese government policy. The author's biography states that she lectures at an Australian university in the field of Chinese language. The reference list of the paper cites many titles by researchers with Asian names who are published in international journals such as *Discourse and Society*. Ideology critique aimed at Chinese institutions appears to be a burgeoning academic field. This critique serves multiple purposes: the career development of its writer; the promotion of her institution as a global player; the political agenda of those in opposition to the Chinese government both internally and externally; and the interests of the owners of the multinational company that publishes the journal who may well have their own reasons for challenging state-owned media institutions.

Conclusion

The concept of critical thinking thus fulfils multiple contradictory functions in relation to diversity in higher education. It functions as marker of difference, as a gate-keeper and as an indicator of the success or otherwise of the academic socialisation project. The challenges faced by international students are undeniable, as is the possibility that some of these challenges are related to the practice of critique. However, explanations which locate the problem within assumed cultural learning patterns have serious limitations. Firstly, such explanations may actually remove incentives to engage with the issue since innate cultural patterns may be seen, by students as much as their teachers, as too powerful to shift. Secondly, they may deflect attention from the struggles of those in the mainstream, positioning them as unproblematic students. Finally, the cultural learning discourse risks reproducing oppositional stereotypes which perpetuate the relations of colonialism, whereby Western academics are easily positioned as enlightened liberatory progressives, freeing cultural others from oppressive thought regimes.

This perspective opens a space for the failure to critique to be understood in terms other than as a cultural deficit. It raises the possibility that what appears as a failure to critique could be a strategy of resistance to the undermining of valued knowledges: a strategy for cultural maintenance. Who knows what silence masks? It would be a mistake to position international students only as powerless subjects of Western colonialist discourses. In the face of practices of critique which subordinate cultural knowledge, it is not surprising if resistance to critique is taken up as a form of critical resistance.

Further analysis is needed to investigate the ways in which critique is identified, taught, learned and assessed in the academy as a whole and within different disciplines. The cultural assumptions and implications of such practices need to be investigated if the internationalised academy is going to foster cultural diversity in the most authentic sense. Such an examination may well reveal that our current means of recognising critical thinking are narrow, limited and exclusive. The circulation of practices of critique through multiple cultural contexts means that critical thinking can never be a single process, despite efforts to package it as such for the global education market.

Changing curriculum and assessment approaches can provide more diverse ways to recognise and develop skills such as critical thinking. Perhaps we could consider inviting our international students to assist us in developing a critique of our own cultural practices, including the practice of critique.

11

Opposing a Rationalist Discourse: Four practitioner stories

DAVID WHITE

David White's writing draws the reader into the power/resistance dilemma of collaborative research: whose research, whose meanings? As with Satterthwaite's chapter, the reader experiences here, in the act of reading, the tensions of negotiated meaning-making involved in the interpretation of a text whose playfulness is, paradoxically, essential. The strangeness in White's account draws the reader into the spaces of where meanings are made, refusing closure, resisting the ownership of educational research in a way that complements the discussion in Quinn's chapter.

I am a practitioner-researcher. I work in a police training college with three colleagues and our role is the education and development of more than twenty training staff. I see two problems with teaching and learning in the police service:

(i) Relationships within the organisation are hierarchical and this is reflected in a transmission-model of teaching;

(ii) The trainers are police officers rather than professional educators. Their short secondments militate against collegiality and the growth of a shared social practice.

My Doctoral research project aimed to address these two issues by engaging the trainers as participants in researching and developing their own practice. The initial stage of the project was to form a core group with my three colleagues. This paper is about the first three months in the life of that core group.

I present it in the form of four stories written from different perspectives – realist, critical, destabilising and reflexive. This is based on ideas by Lather (1991) but developed through the use of just one voice – my own. I use the narratives as positions from which to observe the contrasting and often contradictory themes in my thinking, feeling and action. I did not set out to write stories on different levels, rather I discovered the levels within my writing. I use the word 'position' to indicate how the stories grew out of my writing, rather than out of a classification of my data. I found my self comparing the stories rather than analysing the data (Clough 2001).

Brown and Jones (2001) suggest this approach to narrative in their idea of a chain of stories. The meaning of a narrative is dependent on its place within a temporal sequence, in an analogous way to the relationship between a word and a sentence. Thus my four stories are independent narratives but gain much of their meaning from their interdependence.

I am the narrator. My voice is heard both as reflector in the present and commentator in the past. Other voices are present as echoes, mediated through my field notes and in the way I now choose excerpts to fit the theme I want. The stories are my constructed meanings and interpretations and produce my particular version of events (Chambers 2001). I am the organising consciousness (Clough 2001) and my engagement is both political and moral.

A realist approach: background

I wrote a research report summarising the first three months of the project intended to meet my need to account for what happened. It was written as a factual record based on the assumption of a common level of shared experience. As my writing progressed, the idea of a stable factual foundation became increasingly problematical. I explained the complexity by arguing that the research report was only what *appeared* to happen; the surface appearances concealed something different beneath. These dualisms – appearance/reality and revelation/concealment – are symptomatic of a realist epistemology (Stronach and MacLure 1997).

The realist story is based on my research report.

A realist story: 'I think we're making a mistake'

I designed the project around our work. We would form a core group with the aim of researching our practice as teacher-educators and then engage with the trainers who would research theirs. I envisaged a symbiosis in which two groups researching different things could collaborate to make the other's task possible. The core group would be formed first and would plan how to collaborate with the trainers in what came to be called the 'big group'.

I approached the core group meetings both as chair and facilitator. I anticipated that although a consensus was unlikely we could hope for agreement on a basis for cooperation. I felt it was important to create an atmosphere where doubts and fears could be expressed, and in particular I recognised that my agenda should be supplemented by my colleagues' concerns.

Five meetings were held following the same pattern:

1. My agenda was written up on a white-board and after meetings I added a summary of the debate on each item. I used the board to focus the meetings and as a permanent reminder of progress.

2. I concentrated on a facilitative role, listening carefully and using techniques such as paraphrasing to enable the free expression of views. I gave my opinion when asked, but refrained from advocacy.

3. Each meeting lasted about 1 hour and field notes were written up afterwards. A copy of the field notes was left in the office with an invitation to the others to read and comment.

4. My dual roles of chair and researcher were repeatedly discussed. I encouraged this since it was evidently important to them, and curtailing debate would inhibit sharing and agreement.

The fourth meeting was squeezed into a busy lunch time. Participation was further disrupted by a suggestion that an independent facilitator would be needed to run the big group – it caused some shock and I sensed it was seen as problematical for my research. The meeting ended before the issue was resolved. I considered the possibility that my colleagues were unconsciously resisting progress, but trusted that my facilitative skills would enable concerns to be expressed.

For the fifth meeting I used the white board to highlight the only remaining agenda item – forming the big group. I wrote up anything pertinent from previous meetings, including aim, ideas for action, and anticipated problems. However, my determination to progress was subverted when my colleagues backtracked on the whole idea of a collaborative group. Their consensus was that we should continue to coach trainers individually, though they conceded that relationships could be less hierarchical.

What I had encountered was resistance to collaborative working from colleagues who had a personal investment in their role as experts imparting learning to others. I had expected resistance, but neither so soon nor from this quarter. It seemed to me that I had discovered something important about learning in police cultures.

Comment

It is tempting to discuss what this narrative is *about*; but I prefer to ask *what does it do*?

The realist construction permitted me to explain what happened by blaming the other participants for standing in the way of progress. I used the first person to foreground my role and to minimise the importance of the other characters. Passive constructions were used to refer to events, and pronouns to classify other people. The observer's perspective legitimated objective standards against which notions of 'better' and 'right' could be measured.

I warned my colleagues after the *denouement* 'I think we're making a mistake'. The realist story was complicit in blaming them – '*you* are making the mistake'.

A critical approach: background

My project aimed to counter the organisational hegemony by fostering participation and non-exploitative relationships. It was focussed on emancipation from oppression.

In an early draft I described it as *a peep behind the scenes of the realist story*, reflecting once more the belief that a liberatory narrative explained what was 'really' going on, where the realist story saw only symptoms. This dualism contains the assumption that our conception of what is 'better' can be objectively defined; the two approaches may be antagonistic, but they are both within the discourse of grand narratives (Brown and Jones 2001).

The story is a fictionalisation (Clough 2001), recreating the feel of the final meeting by synthesising material from them all.

A critical story: The board people

The meeting was set for 2.00 pm, but as usual we procrastinated. We found other things to do before sitting down, and once seated, found other things to talk about. I sensed a reluctance to start, as if they were saying 'You want it to start? Then you do it'. I felt my energy drain away.

I had redrawn the white board – setting a new agenda in different coloured pens. I introduced it and invited contributions, but there were none. In fact no one said anything. It felt like my agenda. *Am I the only person interested in this?* I began to feel lonely. When I had planned the meeting I had felt so optimistic – at last nothing stands in the way of deciding some action.

Luke's voice intruded into my thoughts '. . . what stands in the way is the leadership role . . .' and my apparent assumption that there would have to be some leadership '. . . the aim should be to empower others to be leaders . . .' my position is at best the initiator.

I see myself as chair and facilitator, but he is separating these '. . . the facilitator helps the group with finding solutions whereas the chair is a power figure guiding the group . . .'

He was arguing that a group must have the freedom to do what it wants, even if we feel it is wrong. But doesn't this argument just beg the question? We cannot deny our leadership role. The conundrum of leadership is balancing liberation against oppression.

Had we been over these things before? It seemed that we rehearsed them at every meeting.

'. . . the power structure is in our minds and we respond to it sub-consciously . . .' Luke again.

I wondered if subconsciously it was the leadership role that I needed. Do I want to run the big group because I will be in charge, leading it, chairing it? Do I enjoy too much being the focus of attention?

When my thoughts turn outwards to the group once more I find the subject has changed. Luke is describing how he has moved on from the 'old' style of coaching, swapping assessment for co-facilitation.

'. . . a new precedent will be created . . .'

'. . . so do we need to form a group?'

Concern sweeps over me. I want to argue . . . *but we agreed . . . this sets us up as experts . . . we agreed we'd be more democratic . . . we agreed on a group.* But I can't enter the debate; I can't oppose him. I have to chair and facilitate. So I paraphrase him and look to the others.

Stephen.'Our agenda and our language create power for us – we need to have a new process . . .'

Where is this leading? I'm scared. *Our* agenda, he said. But it's clearly my agenda because they wouldn't contribute to it. Are they talking about me? All this talk of power, are they referring to *me?*

'. . . it shouldn't rest on a power structure of formal processes like meetings . . . we must avoid imposing a structure on our plans . . . this implies *not having the group meetings . . .*'

There – he's said it. He doesn't want a group. I tuned out of the meeting. I think I had been expecting it, but it was still a shock. I felt drawn into a confrontation – I want to argue back but the researcher in me is still saying 'hold back'.

My pencil is above the page but I can't move it. Muzac voices. I must do something. I can avoid *arguing* by just giving information. Point out facts – I know I can persuade them. The day can still be saved!

I can't tell you what I said, only what I fantasised later.

Graham was conciliatory. He pointed out that in their suggestion, we could still move towards a group, it would just take longer.

In *their* suggestion? What had I missed? Are they all in this together?

The meeting blurs – them / me / my research. *This isn't going to help you.* I'm not in control of my feelings why is it so hard to handle *how do you feel about that* they're concerned for me this is intense I need a winning argument Graham chokes on a piece of fruit. Someone laughs.

154

And I come to my senses.

I remember feeling resentment. Who are they to question me? I wanted to pretend that it didn't matter so I proposed a cup of tea and then showed my nonchalance by leading the way to the canteen. But everyone knew that it did matter.

I remember once when I was aged five or six being caught disobeying a school rule. I was returned to my class by the head. I was embarrassed and all the other kids at the table wanted to know what I'd done. I didn't want to talk about it. I just wanted them to forget.

That's how I felt at the tea table that afternoon.

Some days later Stephen shared his reflections with me:

> David calls the meeting, sets the agenda and waits/hopes/expects arrangements to be made for a meeting of a wider group . . . We always start with systems and proposals set out on the white board . . . the language of the board shows that we, the board people, have not yet moved away from power, it's language and it's trappings.

Reading this renews my feelings of frustration, and my anger that my actions were so misinterpreted. I wanted a democratic process that was inclusive and enabling. I had acted facilitatively, never imposing anything on them. How could they say these things? Even now I want to argue back. I want to set out my side of the argument to prove they had got it wrong. I want to do it and I feel I could win it. I could change their minds, *Look you've got this wrong. You don't understand what I'm doing. I don't want to experiment on you. I want to work with you. Why don't you want to participate?*

But I can't deny that what they experienced was something quite different. It was no mere disagreement over policy; it was a deeply felt reaction to being railroaded into an idea they did not share. And I am still trying to change their experience by getting them to accept my perception.

Comment

The critical story conceives of power as tangible – possessed by the mighty and inflicted on the oppressed. I was the powerful character and I used my position to impose an idea. It reverses the result of the realist story by blaming me; I am the one who stands in the way of progress by rejecting the 'right' way of working.

But the story acknowledges the voices of the other participants, and in doing so it has to show humility. The privileged status of researcher is given up for a new and more equal position; but with this loss comes a feeling of vulnerability – I am saying to the others, *I am vulnerable too*. Part of the story's meaning is in the action of *being* vulnerable.

A destabilising approach: background

My first two stories have in common the creation of them-and-us roles where 'we' are virtuous and 'they' are to blame. In this approach I challenge the construction of a power/resistance dualism. I use the word 'destabilising' in the sense that it undermines such assumptions (Lather 1991, Brown and Jones 2001).

The realist story deals with events rather than people and the 'I' in the narrative has the feel of an evaluator. In the critical story the characters played the parts of oppressor and oppressed in a liberatory drama (Freire 1970). In this story I locate myself in both camps; I am at the in-between, on the boundary between power and resistance (Stronach and MacLure 1997).

The story mixes extracts from my journal with contemporary reflection.

A destabilizing story: Who pays the bills?

I had been troubled by Bruner's (1990) account of the situated and distributed nature of meaning. It troubled me because whilst I understood the idea of the situatedness of knowledge, I had found it difficult to conceive of distributedness as any thing more than an expansion of the statement that it was shared. It was like saying *widely* situated; but 'widely situated' did not square with the 'cultural nature of knowledge acquisition' (Bruner 1990: 106). So being 'distributed' had to be something to do with the act of acquisition.

I cannot be the sole source of the meaning of something, other people have to share that meaning. However, sharing does not imply that I can just distribute my meaning as if it were the contents of a leaflet. It is in the process of becoming distributed that meaning is shared; in other words meaning is created through distribution rather than being created and then shared by distributing it.

A destabilising story might problematize my other accounts by showing how action was constructed through participation in a social context, rather than through individually reasoned decision making. The rationality of action is questioned. I did not reason and then act, but acted and then rationalised.

In my early journal entries I saw the rational 'me' attempting to make sense of researching in a non-positivist paradigm:

> I guess that I want to look like the professional researcher. Starting a participative research group is not what I thought professional research would look like.

> I want strokes as a thinker and a researcher. Doing the PhD is partly connected to the maintenance of my self-esteem. The trouble is that seeing research in a rational-instrumental mode requires me to be the expert possessing special skills and knowledge, and my research subjects as lesser mortals. I want to research them and then go away with my data to produce my conclusions.

> What makes this so hypocritical is that I want to criticise the organisation for being rational-instrumental! I want to research those aspects of the organisation which get in the way of learning and development – and I'm going to set about it using the same methods as I am criticising.

It was a roller-coaster ride; one day I seemed to have the solution and the next day I had lost it. I spent one weekend producing a version of the proposal, abandoned it on Sunday realising that it was completely wrong, only to readopt it on Tuesday night with just minor changes. Evidently the methodology in the proposal was not the source of the problem; the common denominator was me and how I felt about what I was doing.

Whilst I acknowledged my emotional state I saw it as a separate issue to the design of a methodology; they were related only in as much as one often interfered with the effective pursuit of the other. I had created a person/product dualism and I intended to keep their problems separate. My approach was reinforced by three planning breakthroughs that appeared to work on both levels. I use the word 'breakthrough' because it conveys the sense of an emotional impact as well as a methodological advance. However, dualisms have their own cost of living.

(i) The liberatory motive

In my early writing I shunned the idea of action research because it was not *real* research. Instead I warmed to the related idea of emancipatory research. I was able to distance myself from the former by embracing the latter. This was a self deception. I made myself feel better about doing action research by calling it 'emancipatory' but in liberating participants from the organisation's oppression, I subjected them to my own.

(ii) The research symbiosis

The second breakthrough was recognising the significance of different levels of involvement in the research: myself as researcher, the core group as facilitators and the trainers as practitioners. We have different responsibilities but we achieve democracy through symbiotic interdependence.

However, my application of the idea was flawed because it conflated two separate aspects. Participants come together with different interests in the research – their roles as researcher/practitioner etc – but these are distinct from the activities in which they engage – planning/working/facilitating. Whilst participants' interests in the research are constant, their activities will be interchangeable (Losito *et al* 1998).

I protected my status by retaining control of the expert activities. It relieved the emotional discomfort, but the trade-off was that others' activities were neither democratically allocated nor equal to mine.

(iii) The core group

It was impractical to begin a collaborative group without including my colleagues as equals in the decision-making process. I could only develop new practice through their collaboration, and yet I had no real conception of how to share responsibilities with them.

I was able to unload my emotional stresses through the core group whilst maintaining my superiority by assuming that they had more to learn than me – I was still the expert. The drawback was that their cooperation could last only for as long as they were willing to bear the strain.

I had never resolved my own contradictions about doing collaborative research. I wanted to be both a collaborator and an expert. Each of my breakthroughs was a defensible methodological decision that was subverted to serve my emotional needs; emotionally I was still tied to a positivist paradigm.

Comment

The in-between position at the boundary of a dualism is experienced as a painfulcontradiction. I wanted to be a detached, powerful observer and simultaneously an equal, suffering liberator. The two roles acted reflexively upon each other and produced a third identity, the boundary dweller riven by anxiety (Stronach and MacLure 1997).

The oppositional pairings of word/deed and knowing/feeling are implicated in the story; whatever action is taken its pair comes back to haunt the actor. I like the metaphor of the drama, although the characters now seem much less like actors. (Are they more like real people?) But I want to ask *where are they between performances?* The boundary-dweller seems to have household bills to pay.

A reflexive approach: background

In this approach I reflect-on and move between the other narratives. I pay attention to each and avoid allowing any to dominate (Alvesson and Skoldberg 2000). It is the most contemporary of the approaches and the most optimistic – it contains ideas that contributed to my later attempts at collaborative working.

In an early draft I adopted the title 'My Story' for this narrative, but later added 'No, they're all my stories!' as a reminder to find a better one. I mention this because it revealed an urge to distance myself from the other narratives – particularly the realist story. It was as if I wanted to set aside the uncomfortable and embarrassing parts; to deny that they were really part of me and to portray myself as someone more rational. 'My Story' was to disown the other things that happened.

From the outset I have tried to write from within a non-positivist paradigm, but I still find myself searching for a closure. My stories began to take shape when I stopped trying to *explain* the research, and instead sought to *evoke* it (Lather 1991). Meaning is not discovered in the narrative, but achieved through dialogue with it. Thus, I had to feel that I possessed all the stories – that they were all parts of me. I began to emphasise action and the question, *what do the stories do?* rather than, *what are they about?*

This repossession of my experience is painful because it involves showing you, the reader, my many faults; I seek to evoke what happened through making myself vulnerable. I take the position of learner rather than teacher; of collaborator rather than researcher (Ellis and Bochner 2000).

My last two narratives develop these emerging themes. In the first I search for an elusive new paradigm and in the second I question my drive to explain that experience.

A first reflexive story: The L-shaped room

I share an L-shaped office with my colleagues; the door is on one of the long sides and the windows overlooking the grounds are along the base. My desk and personal space are at the end of the short arm; it is the best position, with more space and privacy than is afforded to the others. I am aware of the status this gives me, in a taken-for-granted sort of way.

An incident caused me to reflect on how I actively use this status symbol rather than just passively benefiting from it. Moving from there would mean more than losing the favoured position, I would have to learn to behave differently. The loss was hard to contemplate because it was linked to my self image.

What surprised me however, was that considering giving up my desk made me much more sensitive to the notion of power in the research relationship. I saw what it would mean, and therefore how important it was, to avoid any sense of power over the other participants. For a tantalising moment I understood what it would feel like to work collaboratively with others, and each time the idea began to drift beyond comprehension I called it back by imagining myself giving up my desk.

It reminded me of Lather's question 'What would a sociological project look like that was not a technology of regulation and surveillance?' (1991 p15). I knew then what it would *feel* like. I would feel challenged to give up some beliefs I have about myself and to give up comfortable ways of acting. This was a different way of understanding 'collaboration'; I understand the word conceptually, and the deed experientially (Palshaugen 2001).

But did I give up my desk? When I reflected on the incident in my journal I was reminded of the notion of a 'sensitising concept' and rather pompously called this way of comprehension a *sensitising action* – an action which sensitises you to new ways of understanding. However, the following day I backtracked and wrote 'I think it would be better called a sensitising *perspective*'. I rationalised not giving up my status by converting the experience into something conceptual.

It was a step that I was not ready to take.

A second reflexive story: The Xmas lights

I made three formal analyses of this phase of my project: the first was the research report; the second was for a research seminar; and the third was for this paper. At each stage I encountered a similar problem and my metaphor for this is *putting the Xmas tree lights back in the box.*

Have you tried it? There's a cardboard notch in the packaging for each of the lights; but you need three hands because after you've slotted a few into place they start popping out randomly. I've found that I can just about manage it – using arms and feet, and then holding the box lid in place with a rubber band. It's not that the lights won't go in – it's that the wires won't let them; or at least, only certain combinations of lights will 'fit' at any one time. The wiring wants to hold the shape of the Xmas tree; and it won't go back into the box without losing it.

One of my peers at the research seminar reported with a practical joviality that he just stuffs the lights into a plastic bag. If the plastic bag were a research metaphor, what would it represent? As a researcher, dare I use a plastic bag for my data?

When I had completed the research report I remember having an uneasy feeling. I had used only a fraction of my material and I sensed there were important things which remained unsaid (or *concealed* – Stronach and MacLure 1997). In the conclusion I wrote:

> This account is personal and idiosyncratic. The outcome was affected by the interaction of four peoples' personalities within a specific work context. In putting it into words I have made choices about the selection and rejection of material and themes; I have simplified, reduced and re-presented.

I think that I wrote this because I felt inept about leaving so much hidden. I could justify 'simplifying, reducing and re-presenting' by confessing what I had done – and that made it feel all right.

For the research seminar I wrote and rejected two plans over a three-month period. Each time the material defied my best efforts to synthesise a concise account that *said it all*. I remember knocking my head with frustration and urging 'Come on! If you just work hard enough you'll find *the order* there'. In time, I began to comprehend that discovering the perfect formulation was not really the problem; it was that presenting it to my peers as such would be to *act* inconsistently with the collaborative ideal that had motivated me. I felt that there was something fundamentally ethical about *doing* research in collaborative ways. Thus in the final plan I decided not to 'present my findings' but rather to use a number of short excerpts to evoke discussion.

I wrote this story during my third phase of analysis. I discussed it with Luke and following one such conversation I reflected:

> I've just realised that my current piece of writing is creating in me the same struggles with positivism as I have experienced in other ways. I want to be seen as logical and analytical; as I have just said to Luke, *I want to be seen as a guy who can really put a piece of writing together*. It seems to both take a self-awareness and an effort of will to resist the urge to rationalise an account.

I found that learning to write and act within a different discourse entailed the emotional difficulty of discovering new sources of self affirmation – understanding how to live a collaborative relationship. I could read something and understand it on a conceptual level, but knowing it at the level of action was to experience it as a way of living. There was an ethical dimension to the lived experience that was opaque to my armchair logic.

So where are my lights now? Are they back in the box anyway? I invite you to share my anxiety.

12

Creative Pedagogies of Resistance in Post Compulsory (teacher) Education

KEN GALE

Ken Gale proposes a creative resistance to dominant policy technologies in post compulsory teacher education. He proposes a situated, participative and discursive approach to learning which echoes Quinn's arguments, while his exploration of radical uncertainty links his argument to those of both Quinn and Atkinson. Gale takes us firmly back into the territories of the unknown visited earlier in White's chapter, and suggests that, by relinquishing control and opening ourselves to the unexpected, we have much to learn which can open up new possibilities for professional identity and educational practice.

Introduction

In this chapter, I present the argument that radical, discursive and essentially creative pedagogies of resistance are required within post compulsory teacher education to address some of the effects of the policy initiatives that currently impact on the post compulsory sector. I propose creative practices which offer a resistance to the prescriptive implementation of narrow outcomes-driven programmes that privilege technocratic rather than educative models of practice, and discuss these practices in relation to a rethinking of structure and agency as a dynamic process rather than a static binary opposition. I suggest that it is within this critical and dynamic context that emerging creative pedagogies can be used to reconfigure existing notions of professional identity and practice style, and offer Baudelaire's image of the flâneur as a metaphor for the creative practitioner who is open to unintended and unexpected discoveries as a means of teaching and learning. The creative practices that are being proposed here will promote a recognition of contingency and encourage active processes of problematisation: if more questions are raised than answers provided by this chapter then it will be seen as having had some success.

Policy Technologies?

This chapter is set in the context of what Ball (2001b) describes as the 'policy technologies' that currently influence teaching and learning in Britain and elsewhere. For Ball, these interrelated and interdependent policy moves help create not only the organising principles and processes of education reform, but also what he refers to as the 'assumptive worlds' in which professional practice is carried out. These worlds, he argues, are constituted by related sets of norms, values and attitudes. On this account, policy is not only an agent for generating curriculum change but also, and perhaps more significantly, it is seen as being responsible for establishing a framework of legitimacy for professional identity and practice style.

The emergence of these policy technologies in Post Compulsory Education and Training in recent years can be seen in the role in policy making played by a number of major funding bodies, such as the Further Education Funding Council (FEFC); more recently the Learning and Skills Council (LSC); and the Higher Education Funding Council (HEFC). The regimes set up by these bodies have had a substantial influence upon curriculum design and delivery, the principles and characteristics of teaching and the promotion of learning within a strictly vocational context. As a consequence, post compulsory education has experienced a shift of focus toward issues of quality assurance, clearly prescribed sets of standards and specific requirements for teaching and learning practice. This has also had a significant impact upon teacher education and training within the post compulsory sector. The Dearing Report (1997), sponsored by the government as part of a reconceptualisation of higher education, has led to the emergence of professional bodies such as the Institute for Learning and Teaching (ILT) in higher education and the Further Education National Training Organisation (FENTO) in further education. Whilst Dearing stressed the need for the existence of practitioner organisations that are distanced from regulatory and funding bodies, it is clear that the role played by organisations such as ILT and FENTO has been influenced by these bodies. The expressed purposes and aims of these organisations are, through the setting of standards, to improve the quality of teaching and learning in the post compulsory sector, thus contributing to the creation and maintenance of policy technologies.

These policy technologies can be examined in at least two ways. First, they can be examined in relation to the way in which they overtly influence the manner in which curriculum development is carried out, teaching styles are chosen, learning outcomes are linked to assessment and so on. Second, they can be examined in relation to the way in which they covertly influence the thinking, attitudes and values, in short, the professional identity and practice style, of all those involved in education. While these two perspectives could be seen as direct representations of structure and agency, my aim here is propose a creative approach to post compulsory teacher education which challenges what Ball refers to as 'the simplicities of the structure/agency dichotomy' (1994: 14).

Structure versus Agency?

Foucault moves away from the structure/agency binary when he describes his mode of working (1991b: 90–91):

> My work takes place between unfinished abutments and anticipatory strings of dots. I like to open out a space of research, try it out, then if it doesn't work try again somewhere else. On many points . . . I am still working and don't yet know whether I am going to get anywhere. What I say ought to be taken as 'propositions', 'game openings' where those who may be interested are invited to join in; they are not meant to be seen as dogmatic assertions that have to be taken or left en bloc . . .

Foucault is not simply proposing that structure influences or determines agency, as is suggested by traditional structuralist models, but that structure appears to exchange with the agent in an intricate, complex and sometimes volatile dynamic. What Foucault's image suggests is an assertive agency operating for, against and within a fluid and responsive pattern of relations. Deleuze and Guattari (1988) refer to processes of 'territorialisation' and 're-territorialisation' to describe the way in which such a dynamic can be conceptualised, drawing on their image of the rhizome to represent the unpredictable and organic growth of ideas or practices with no clear or definable structure. Rather than policy technologies, as an over-arching structure, being seen to territorialise individuals within a framework of disempowering passivity, Deleuze and Guattari suggest a dynamic in which individuals respond to and re-constitute the territory of which, crucially, they are a part. Foucault's 'propositions' and 'game openings' can be seen as creative strategies that can provide the opportunity for new structures or territories to emerge.

Such rhizomatic developments within the post compulsory sector, conceived in terms of propositions and game openings, can facilitate paradigm shifts (Kuhn, 1962) which invite innovative teaching practices, risk taking curriculum strategies and critically reflexive methodologies. These creative practices invite practitioners to acknowledge contingency and to reflexively encounter knowledge as it is discursively constructed across a multiplicity of sites. Bruner (1996) has demonstrated that, within these sites, emergent, competing and shared narratives all contribute in highly discursive ways to the construction of knowledge and learning within a complex culture of education. In this paradigm, knowledge does not come packaged with standards and endorsed by policies, but is constructed and contested by participants in the learning process, for example through the recognition of critical incidents (Tripp, 1993) in teaching and learning. For Tripp, it is through the attaching of particular significance to specific events or moments that new developments in understanding and practice emerge. These critical incidents provide for the growth of learning around significant nodes or points: a model which owes more to the rhizome than to the learning ladder or framework of standards. From another perspective, West (1999) describes the development of an 'intellectual' professional practice in post compulsory education which is not based on rational thinking, but which represents the confluence of the adult learner's personal desire with her/his emerging voice as a practitioner. Here, again, is a rhizomatic model of learning whose openness and potential for innovation and change can generate pedagogies of resistance to dominant modes of practice.

Deleuze and Guattari suggest that the rhizome 'ceaselessly establishes connections between semiotic chains [and] organisations of power'. They argue that 'there is no language in itself, nor are there any linguistic universals, only a throng of dialects, patois, slangs, and specialised languages,' proposing a resistance to a 'power takeover by a dominant language within a political multiplicity' (1988: 7–8). Creative pedagogies of resistance, in recognising that language is never closed upon itself, must involve the use of reflexive and deconstructive strategies as a means of opening up new possibilities in a varied and complex postmodern world: a world that is characterised by complexity, diversity and pluralism. In an evaluation of contemporary post compulsory education, Edwards expresses disquiet regarding the way in which the landscapes of learning have previously been mapped. He argues that a 'differentiated and bounded field of adult education' is being displaced by a more 'diverse moorland' (1997: 67) signifying rich metaphorical spaces of exploration in which substantial interplay and exchange between discourses can occur. This diverse moorland is clearly radically different from the cultivated and regulated fields of a controlled learning economy, and this diversity – of teachers, learners, contexts and opportunities – offers new opportunities for development. At present, post compulsory teacher education appears to function within a clearly demarcated field of policy and practice, managed, legitimated, examined and evaluated in terms of its own policy technologies. Edwards suggests, however, that 'not only are the boundaries shifting and becoming more permeable, but the structuring metaphors of boundedness are themselves questionable' (*ibid*: 68).

The paradigm shift being considered here, then, may involve a redefinition of the whole field of post compulsory teacher education, in which the social construction of knowledge takes place across a diversity of sites in which learning might be differentiated, collaborative, contested and characterised by uniqueness. As Edwards says, 'On the moorland, there is more open-ended exploration, a searching for new routes to travel through a complex and uncertain ecology and archaeology' (*ibid*: 69). In these places of open-ended exploration, the relationship between structure and agency becomes both complex and uncertain.

The Flâneur?

A metaphor for the discovery of the unexpected through open-ended exploration can be found in the 19th century poetic writing of Baudelaire (see the *Collected Works*, 1975). Baudelaire's image of the poet is embedded within the concept of the flâneur, whose mixture of ennui, disgust and exhilaration defies both structure and boundaries. The flâneur's activities, characterised by strolling and looking, can in themselves be seen as a form of resistance, and adopting the professional identity of the flâneur and the practice style of flânerie offers new perspectives on post compulsory teacher education. The aimless wandering of the flâneur combines the ennui and disgust arising from existing configurations and arrangements with the excitement of exploring the new and the unknown. The figure and the activity are increasingly used by commentators in an attempt to gain an understanding of some of the implications of modernity and post modernity (Tester, 1994).

The concept of the flâneur can be seen reflected in Paul Auster's book *The New York Trilogy* (1987). Here the central character Quinn, a private investigator, is given the task of following Stillman, an old man whose behaviour is shrouded in mystery.

> What Stillman did on these walks remained something of a mystery to Quinn. He could, of course, see with his own eyes what happened, and all these things he dutifully recorded in his red note-book. But the meaning of these things continued to elude him. Stillman never seemed to be going anywhere in particular, nor did he seem to know where he was. (1987: 58)

Auster describes Quinn as being used to wandering. 'His excursions through the city had taught him to understand the connectedness of inner and outer. Using aimless motion as a technique of reversal, on his best days he could bring the outside in and thus usurp the sovereignty of inwardness' (*ibid*: 61). Despite this contemplative acuity, Quinn suffers the ennui of an apparently aimless pursuit when, after many days of following, he begins to detect what appears to be a pattern to Stillman's wanderings. In walking the streets he traces the form of letters and spells out words to construct a particular phrase. Quinn is stunned and excited to discover that Stillman's wanderings appear to be purposeful despite their random appearance.

He wondered if Stillman had sat down each night in his room and plotted his course for the following day or whether he had improvised as he had gone along. He also wondered what purpose this writing served in Stillman's mind. Was it some note to himself, or was it intended as a message to others? (*ibid*: 71)

Auster's tale demonstrates that although structures may be perceived to exist in a diversity of places and can be discovered, or constructed, in many, often obtuse ways, they are also open to multiple interpretations. Thus the trainee teacher – and the teacher-trainer – in post compulsory teacher education can, like Quinn, discover the unexpected within the unintended, and can, without knowing where he or she is going, discover new meanings, questions and directions.

Even when Quinn appears to 'have something' on his 'suspect' he realises that the patterns and structures he feels he has detected may be seen to exist in a number of dimensions and levels and be interpreted in a variety of ways. Quinn's puzzled contemplation of the structure that appears to frame the behaviour of his quarry, and his concern over the discovery that Stillman's patterns are being traced intentionally, demonstrate the problems that are associated with the implementation of simplistic interpretation. Quinn will gain insufficient satisfaction from appealing to the explanatory dualisms of Cartesian thought. Opposing conceptualisations of structure and agency, object and subject, cause and effect and reality and representation all dissolve within the complexity of the puzzle that confronts him. The solution, if there is one, is far more complex, diverse and contingent in quality.

Exploring these complexities takes the flâneur into Wittgenstein's world of language games. 'Our language can be seen as an ancient city: a maze of little streets and squares, of old and new houses, and of houses with additions from various periods, and this surrounded by a multitude of new boroughs with straight regular streets and uniform houses.' (1978: sec.18, p8) He suggests that we can only begin to understand this landscape through exploration, by wandering through the city to discover its intricate and changing detail. It is a practice that can be exciting, enjoyable and educational. Auster's character Quinn enjoys the possibilities that are offered by his wandering. 'Nearly every day, rain or shine, hot or cold, he would leave his apartment to walk through the city – never really going anywhere – but simply going wherever his legs happened to take him' (*ibid*: 3). He is exhilarated and invigorated by the experience. 'There is something nice about being in the dark, he discovers, something thrilling about not knowing what is going to happen next. It keeps you alert, he thinks, and there's no harm in that, is there? Wide awake and on your toes, taking it all in, ready for anything' (*ibid*: 152).

The flâneur exemplifies the complex feelings of anxiety, wonderment and discovery associated with learning, fuelled by a volatile mixture of disgust, curiosity and a desire to uncover something different, something new. The terrain which the flâneur explores is like that described by Plant (1998) in her discussion of the intricate networks and matrices of texts. When Plant describes the mainstream and backwaters, the currents and eddies of written language she characterises the terrain in which flâneurs can indulge their inquisitive journeying: a terrain which might provide fertile ground for a creative pedagogy of resistance.

> Distinctions between the main bodies of texts and all their peripheral detail – indices, headings, prefaces, dedications, appendices, illustrations, references, notes, and diagrams – have long been integral to orthodox conceptions of non-fiction books and articles. Authored, authorised, and authoritative, a piece of writing is its own mainstream. Its asides are backwaters which might have been – and often are – compiled by anonymous editors, secretaries, copyists, and clerks, and while they may well be providing crucial support for a text which they also connect to other sources, resources, and leads, they are also sidelined and downplayed.
>
> (Plant 1998: 9)

The teacher as flâneur, then, wanders the backwaters to discover what might have been sidelined and downplayed. This pursuit has less to do with direction than with connection: as Foucault puts it, 'We are at a moment, I believe, when our experience of the world is less that of a long life developing through time than that of a network that connects points and intersects with its own skein' (1998: 237). Plant draws on Foucault's image of intertextuality:

> The frontiers of a book are never clear-cut: beyond the title, the first lines, and the last full stop, beyond its internal configuration and its

autonomous form, it is caught up in a system of references to other books, other texts, other sentences: it is a node within a network.

(Foucault in Plant 1997/98: 10)

Similar in spirit to Foucault's genealogical methodology, flânerie will resist the 'authored, authorised, and authoritative' mainstream and inquisitively pursue and examine those passages and byways that have been ignored and allowed to become obscured. The flâneur not only inquisitively and critically examines undisclosed or hidden pathways but also slows the pace of these curious investigations down to suit the intensity of observation and analysis. By making the familiar strange, the flâneur 'opens up an attention to detail, grain, and complexity' (Dean, 1994: 93–4). In this light, learning outcomes, lesson plans and prescriptive schemes of work are themselves made strange, and become part of a complex and open-ended terrain in which each direction, however obscure its significance might at first appear to be, yields its own rewards. This exploration will involve radical interpretation and re-conceptualisation of conventional analyses and practices: practitioners engaged in creative pedagogies of resistance will benefit from an awareness of Baudrillard's 'precession of simulacra' in which the signs, images and visual representations of everyday life construct us in particular ways. We might explore ways in which to defy the process by which 'the map . . . precedes the territory . . . it is the map that engenders the territory' (1983: 361). Or we might construct new maps which take us on new journeys, as well as analysing the ways in which existing maps, such as curriculum models, schemes of work and lesson plans might be seen to influence the journeys we take in specific practice contexts.

Emerging Practice Styles?

The exploration and analysis of old maps and terrains and the creation of new ones gives rise to new professional identities and practice styles, characterised by uncertainty, contingency, and the need, in Derrida's terms (1978) to keep the language by which they are framed 'under erasure': used but crossed out to demonstrate both its necessity and its inadequacy. Such identities and practice styles echo Schön's idea of a 'nonrational intuitive artistry' (1983: 239), or what Bleakley (1999) describes as a 'holistic reflexivity'.

Irigaray (1974) writes of listening with another ear to words that cannot be heard, and of getting rid of words which create their own boundaries. She is describing *parler-femme*, the empathic communication between women, but this indeterminate text, these inaudible words, become accessible within teaching and learning once we step outside the boundaries of structures, standards and schemes. They are:

> . . . contradictory words, somewhat mad from the standpoint of reason, inaudible for whoever listens with ready-made grids, with a fully elaborated code in hand. For in what she says too, at least when she dares, woman is constantly touching herself. She steps ever so slightly aside from herself with a murmur, an exclamation, a whisper, a sentence left unfinished . . . When she returns it is to set off again from elsewhere . . . One would have to listen with another ear, as if hearing an 'other meaning' always in the process of weaving itself, of embracing itself with words; but also of getting rid of words in order not to become fixed, congealed in them.
>
> (1974: 29)

Irigaray's *parler-femme* suggests ways in which collaborative teacher education practices could acknowledge and implement discussion and analysis in innovative and creative ways, using emotion and feeling in language as a complement to the orthodoxy of more positivistic practices. The *frisson* within the close and dynamic relationship that Irigaray's writing evokes is far removed from the 'ready-made grids' and 'fully elaborated codes' that traditional teacher education practices are often constrained to develop and maintain.

Flânerie suggests a pedagogy of wandering that is not only inquisitive and curious but which can also be cumulative, digressive and rhetorical. The flâneur is constantly addressing and re-addressing learning and knowledge in the encounter with new, different and frequently divergent experiences. As a practice, flânerie possesses aspirations of openness, never closure, and it is through this resistance to closure, through close attention to the unknown and the unexpected, and through the re-envisioning of the terrain of teaching and learning that creative pedagogies of resistance can emerge.

The Contributors

Elizabeth Atkinson is a Reader in the School of Education and Life-long Learning at the University of Sunderland. Her published work spans a wide spectrum, including critical analyses of educational research, policy and practice, and postmodern perspectives on discourses of education, identity and social justice. She takes a particular interest in bringing together conflicting perspectives in educational and social research, and in unsettling certainties within contemporary educational discourse.

Elizabeth Burn qualified as a primary teacher in 1970 in the North East of England. She has combined teaching pupils aged 3–11 years with bringing up her own 3 children. After a period of deputy head-ship and advisory work, she moved into teacher training in 1991. She is currently a Senior Lecturer in Primary Mathematics in the Department of Education at London Metropolitan University. Her research interests are concerned with equity work in education.

Julia Clarke is Research Fellow in the Open University's Faculty of Education and Language Studies, employed initially to pilot a methodology for the study of flexibility in further education. She is currently engaged in several small-scale research projects on a theme of 'working around literacy', in which she is exploring the use of visual approaches to research and representation.

Helen Colley: Formerly a care assistant, bus driver, factory worker and careers adviser, Dr Helen Colley is now Senior Research Fellow and Academic Co-ordinator at the Lifelong Learning Institute, University of Leeds. Her research on mentoring has won wide acclaim, including the John Tunnadine Prize and the British Educational Research Association Award for Best PhD Dissertation.

She is also a Fellow of the National Institute for Careers Education and Counselling.

Richard Edwards is Professor of Education at the University of Stirling, Scotland. Prior to that he worked at the Open University, where he directed the project, Flexibility in Further Education: a Mapping Study. He has written and researched extensively on lifelong learning, postmodernism and poststructuralism. His most recent book (with Robin Usher) is *Globalisation and Pedagogy: Space, Place and Identity*.

Terry Finnigan has worked in Further Education and Higher Education as a Study Support tutor for over twenty years. She gained a degree in Sociology in 1978 from Salford University, England and an MA in Language in the Multi-cultural Community, from Thames Valley University, London in 2000. She is currently working part-time at the London Metropolitan University and the London Institute as a Senior Lecturer in Study Support. Her research interests include language, identity and refugee teaching.

Ken Gale is a Senior Lecturer in the Faculty of Arts and Education at the University of Plymouth, teaching on a range of post compulsory education courses from Certificate to Masters level. His particular interest lies within the philosophy of education and the study of post structural theory as it applies to teacher education. His published work covers human relations theory, triadic assessment and creative practice in teacher education.

Roger Harrison is a Lecturer in the Faculty of Education and Language Studies at the Open University. He teaches on the Masters Programme in Education (Lifelong Learning) and has written and researched on lifelong learning, adult guidance, professional development and self managed learning. Before joining the Faculty he was involved in community education initiatives aimed at widening access to learning.

Dennis Hayes is Head of the Department of Post-Compulsory Education at Canterbury Christ Church University College. Along with his colleagues, he wrote a best selling textbook, *Teaching and Training in Post-Compulsory Education*. He edited (with Robin Wynyard) a collection of essays on *The McDonaldization of Higher Education*, and is completing a related book, *Defending Higher Education, From Itself: the crisis of confidence in the academy.*

David Hursh is Associate Professor at the University of Rochester, Rochester, New York. His political organizing, research and writing focus on the theory and practice of developing democratic schools through changing curriculum, teaching, and assessment. His publications include the book *Democratic Social Education: Social Studies for Social Change* (co-edited with Wayne Ross) and articles in *Theory and Research in Social Education, Discourse,* and elsewhere.

Susan Nichols is a researcher at the Centre for Literacy, Policy and Learning Cultures at the University of South Australia where she also teaches and supervises postgraduate students. She is interested in the production of knowledge through the discursive practices of education, particularly the practices of textual production. Susan investigates in diverse educational sites including universities, schools, kindergartens and homes and regularly publishes her work.

Jocey Quinn is Research Fellow at the Institute for Access Studies, Staffordshire University. Her research interests include the construction of knowledge and subjectivity, interdisciplinary methodology and changing intergenerational perspectives on knowledge. Her book, *Powerful Subjects* (2003), on the mass participation of women in HE, is based on her PhD from Lancaster University.

Fiona Reeve is a Lecturer in Lifelong Learning at The Open University, where she contributes to the distance learning 'Masters in Education (Lifelong Learning)'. Her research interests include work-based learning, flexibility in further education and the boundaries between experiential and formal learning. She is currently undertaking research into the implementation of work-based learning programmes within higher education in the UK.

Stephen Rowland has taught and researched in primary schools, in in-service education and in the field of higher education. His books, including *The Enquiring Classroom* (1984), *The Enquiring Tutor* (1993) and *The Enquiring University Teacher* (2000), reflect his commitment to forms of education in which teachers and learners are engaged in critically interpreting their human and physical world. Since 2000 he has held the Chair in Higher Education at University College London.

Jerome Satterthwaite teaches in the Graduate School of the University of Plymouth after working for some years as Teacher Fellow in the School of Cultural Studies at Leeds Metropolitan University. He is the organiser of the Discourse, Power, Resistance conferences hosted by the Graduate School at Plymouth. He has a life-long hatred of long words and continues to research their baleful effect on the learning experiences of adults.

David White has been involved in police officer training for 14 years, and latterly in educating police-trainers. His background is in psycho-dynamic psychology and his Doctoral research with The University of Plymouth is into collaborative learning. He sees teaching as a representation of knowledge that embodies moral responsibilities to others. This shapes his pedagogic practice and has led his towards narrative and fiction as research methodologies.

Bibliography

Adonis, A (1998) *A Class Act*. London: Penguin

Ainley, P (1994) *Degrees of Difference*. London: Lawrence and Wishart

Ainley, P and Bailey, B (1997) *The Business of Learning*. London: Cassell

Alexander, D and Rivzi, F (1993) Education, markets and the contradictions of Asia-Australia relations, in: Bella, M *et al* (eds) *Higher Education in Transition: Working papers of the Higher Education Policy Project*. Brisbane: University of Queensland

Almond, B (1991) Human Bonds, in: Almond, B and Hill, D (eds) *Applied Philosophy: morals and metaphysics in contemporary debate*. London: Routledge

Alvesson, M and Skoldberg, K (2000) *Reflexive Methodology*. Sage: London

Annan, N G (1999) *The Dons: mentors, eccentrics and geniuses*. London: Harper Collins

Apple, M (2001) *Educating the 'Right' Way: Markets, Standards, God, and Inequality*. New York: Routledge

Armitage, A, Bryant, R, Dunnill, R, Hammersley, M, Hayes, D, Hudson, A and Lawes, S (2003) *Teaching and Training in Post-Compulsory Education (2nd edn)*. Milton Keynes: Open University Press

Armstrong, M (1980) *Closely Observed Children: the diary of a primary school classroom*. London: Writers and Readers

Atkinson, D (1999) TESOL and Culture, in: *TESOL Quarterly* 33(4): 625–654

Atkinson, E (2000a) Critical dissonance and critical schizophrenia: the struggle between policy delivery and policy critique, in: *Research Intelligence, 73*, November 2000: 14–17

Atkinson, E (2000b) The promise of uncertainty: education, postmodernism and the politics of possibility, in: *International Studies in Sociology of Education, 10*(1): 81–99

Atkinson, E (2000c) What can postmodern thinking do for educational research? Paper presented at the annual conference of the American Educational Research Association, New Orleans, 24th–28th April 2000

Atkinson E (2000d) In Defence of Ideas, or Why 'What Works' is Not Enough, in: *British Journal of Sociology of Education, 21*(3): 317–330

Atkinson, E (2001) Deconstructing boundaries: out on the inside? in: *International Journal of Qualitative Studies in Education, 14*(3): 307–316

Atkinson, E (2002a) The responsible anarchist: postmodernism and social change, in: *British Journal of Sociology of Education, 23*(1): 73–87

Atkinson, E (2002b) Troubling certainty in educational research. Unpublished critical analysis for PhD by publication, University of East Anglia. Norwich: UEA

Auster, P (1987) *The New York Trilogy*. London: Faber and Faber

Australian, The (2001) 'Test of reasoning abilities to clear up doubts' 27th September: 43. Accessed on-line www.theaustralian.news.com

Avis, J (1996) The Enemy Within: Quality and Managerialism in Education, in: Avis, J *et al Knowledge and Nationhood: Education, Politics and Work*. London: Cassell

Avis, J (1998) The Myth of Post-Fordist Society, in: Avis, J, Bloomer, M, Esland, G, Gleeson, D and Hodkinson, P *Knowledge and Nationhood: Education, Politics and Work*. London: Cassell

Avis, J (1999) 'Shifting Identity: new conditions and the transformation of practice – teaching within post-compulsory education', in: *Journal of Vocational Education and Training*, 51(2): 245–263

Avis, J (2000) Policing the subject: Learning outcomes, managerialism and research in PCET, in: *British Journal of Educational Studies*, 48(1): 38–57

Ball, S (1994) *Education Reform*. Buckingham: Open University Press

Ball, S (1995) Intellectuals or Technicians? The Urgent Role of Theory in Educational Studies, in: *British Journal of Educational Studies* 43(3): 255–271

Ball, S (2001a)Speaking back to evidence. Opening address to the annual meeting of the Society for Educational Studies, Institute of Education, London, 15th November 2001

Ball, S (2001b) *Performativity and Fabrication in the Education Economy*: A lecture given at University of Exeter School of Education, 29th May 2001

Barry, A, Osborne, T and Rose, N (1996) *Foucault and Political Reason*: *Liberalism, Neo-Liberalism, and the Rationalities of Government*. Chicago: University of Chicago Press

Barthes, R (1977) *Image – Music – Text* (trans S. Heath). Glasgow: Fontana/Collins

Beavers, A *Emmanuel Levinas and the Prophetic Voice of Postmodernity*. See http://cedar.evansville.edu/˜tb2/trip/prophet.htm

Baudelaire, C P (Ed. Claude Pichois) (1975) *Ouevres Complètes*. Paris: Editions Gallimard

Baudrillard J (1983) *Simulations*. New York: Semiotext(e)

Becher, T (1989) *Academic Tribes and Territories*. Milton Keynes: Society for Research into Higher Education and Open University Press

Beck, U (1992) *Risk Society. Towards a New Modernity*. London: Sage

Berliner, D and Biddle, B (1995) *The Manufactured Crisis: Myths, Frauds, and the Attack on America's Public Schools*. Reading, MA: Addison Wesley

Bhopal, K (1994) The Influence of Feminism on Black Women in the Higher Educational Curriculum, in: Davis, S, Lubelska, C, and Quinn, J (eds), *Changing the Subject*. London: Taylor and Francis

Blackmore, J (2000) 'Globalization: A Useful Concept for Feminists Rethinking Theory and Strategies in Education', in: Torres, C A and Burbules, N (eds) *Globalization and Education: Critical Perspectives*. New York: Routledge

Bibliography

Blackstone, T (2001) Why learn? Higher education in a learning society, in: *Higher Education Quarterly* 55(2): 175–84

Blair, T (1998) *The Third Way: New Politics for the New Century*. London: Fabian Society

Bleakley, A (1999) From Reflective Practice to Holistic Reflexivity, in: *Studies in Higher Education* 24(3): 315–330

Bloomer, M (1996) Education for Studentship, in: Avis, J *et al Knowledge and Nationhood: Education, Politics and Work*. London: Cassell

Bloomer, M (1997) *Curriculum Making in Post-16 Education – The Social Conditions of Studentship*. London: Routledge

Bohman, J (1999) 'Practical Reason and Cultural Constraint: Agency in Bourdieu's Theory of Practice', in: Shusterman, R *Bourdieu: A Critical Reader*. Oxford: Blackwell

Bourdieu, P (1998) *Acts of Resistance: Against the Tyranny of the Market*. New York: The New Press

Bourdieu, P (1986) *Distinction: A Social Critique of the Judgement of Taste*. London: Routledge

Bourdieu, P (1990) *Homo Academicus*. Cambridge: Polity

Bourdieu, P (1991) *Language and Symbolic Power*. Cambridge: Polity

Bourdieu, P (1993) *Sociology in Question*. London: Sage

Bourdieu, P *et al* (1994) *Academic Discourse: Linguistic Misunderstanding and Professorial Power*. Cambridge: Polity

Boyer, E L (1990) *Scholarship Reconsidered: Priorities of the Professoriate*. New York: Harper Collins

Bracey, G (2002) The 12th Bracey Report on the Condition of Education, in: *Phi Delta Kappan* October: 135: 150

Brice Heath, S (1991) *Children of Promise: Literate Activity in Linguistically and Culturally Diverse Classrooms*. Washington DC: National Education Association

Britzman, D (1995) The question of belief: writing poststructural ethnography, in: *International Journal of Qualitative Studies in Education,* 8(3): 229–238

Britzman, D P and Dippo, D (2000) On the future of awful thoughts in teacher education, in: *Teaching Education,* 11(1): 31–37

Brown, T and Jones, L (2001) *Action Research and Postmodernism: congruence and critique*. Buckingham: Open University Press

Bruner, J (1979) *On Knowing: Essays for the left hand*. (Expanded edition) Cambridge, MA and London: The Belknap Press of Harvard University Press. (Original edition 1962)

Bruner, J (1990) *Acts of Meaning*. Cambridge Mass: Harvard University Press

Bruner, J (1996) *The Culture of Education*. London: Harvard University Press

Bryan, J (1998) Review of Reeves, F (ed) (1997) *Further Education as Economic Regeneration: The Starting Point*. Bilston: Bilston Community College and Education and Now Books, in: *Youth and Policy,* (61) Autumn 1998: 99–101

Burn, E (1999) Maths Stories, *Primary Teaching Studies* 10 (2)

Burn, E (2000) 'You Won't Want to get Your Hands Dirty': An Early Years teacher reflecting on her training experience, in: *Education and Social Justice* 3(1) Autumn: 59–64

Burn, E (2001) Battling Through the System: a working-class teacher in an inner-city primary school, in: *International Journal of Inclusion Education*. 5(1): 85–92

Butler, J Performativity's Social Magic, in: Shusterman, R (1999) *Bourdieu: A Critical Reader*. Oxford: Blackwell

Calman, K C (2000) *A Study of Story Telling Humour and Learning in Medicine*. London: Nuffield Trust

Campaign for Fiscal Equity (2002) Status of CFE v. State of New York. Retrieved June 2, 2002 from www.cfequity.org

Capizzi, E, Carter, J and Davies, P (1998) Making sense of credit: FE staff managing change, in: *Journal of Access and Credit Studies*, 1(1): 40–52

Caputo, J D (1993) *Against Ethics: Contributions to a poetics of obligation with constant reference to deconstruction*. Bloomington: Indiana University Press

Carr, D (2000) *Professionalism and Ethics in Teaching*. London: Routledge

Carr, W (1995) Education and Democracy: confronting the postmodern challenge, in: *Journal of Philosophy of Education*. 29(1): 75–91

Chambers, P (2001) *Different Strokes for Different Folks: an international perspective on storying as a methodological tool*. Paper delivered at the British Educational Research Association Conference, 2001

Clark, B R (2000) College Entrepreneurialism in Proactive Universities: Lessons from Europe, in: *Change,* January/February: 10–19

Clough, P (2001) *Fiction and the Narratives of Educational Research*. Paper delivered at the British Educational Research Association Conference 2001

Cochran-Smith, M and Paris, C L (1995) Mentor and mentoring: did Homer have it right? In: Smyth, J (ed) *Critical Discourses on Teacher Development*. London: Cassell

Coffey, A (1999) *The Ethnographic Self*. London: Sage

Cohen, R (1994) *Elevations: The Height of the Good in Rozenweig and Levinas*. Chicago: University of Chicago Press

Cole, M (1999a) Professional issues in Initial Teacher Education: What can be done and what should be done? in: *Education and Social Justice*. 2(1)

Cole, M (1999b) (ed) *Professional Issues for Teachers and Student Teachers*. London: David Fulton Publishers

Colley, H (2000a) *Mind the Gap: Policy Goals and young people's resistance in a mentoring scheme*. Paper given at British Educational Research Association Annual Conference, Cardiff University, 7 September

Colley, H (2000b) Deconstructing 'realism' in career planning: how globalisation impacts on vocational guidance, in: Roberts, K (ed) *Careers Guidance Constructing the Future: A Global Perspective*. Richmond: Trotman/Institute of Careers Guidance

Colley, H (2001a) Righting re-writings of the myth of Mentor: a critical perspective on career guidance mentoring, in: *British Journal of Guidance and Counselling* 29(2): 177–198

Colley, H (2001b) *Unravelling Myths of Mentor: Power Dynamics of Mentoring*

Relationships with 'Disaffected' Young People. Unpublished PhD thesis, The Manchester Metropolitan University

Colley, H (2002) A Rough Guide to the history of mentoring from a Marxist feminist perspective, in: *Journal of Education for Teaching* 28(3): 247–263

Colley, H. (2003 in press) Engagement mentoring for 'disaffected' youth: a new model of mentoring for social inclusion, in: *British Educational Research Journal*

Colley, H (forthcoming) *Mentoring for Social Inclusion: A Critical Approach to Nurturing Mentor Relationships.* London: Routledge Falmer

Colley, H and Hodkinson, P (2001) Problems with 'Bridging The Gap': the reversal of structure and agency in addressing social exclusion, in: *Critical Social Policy* 21(3): 337–361

Collins, J and Lear, J (1995) *Chile's Free-Market Miracle: A Second Look*, Oakland, CA: The Institute for Food and Development Policy

Conrad, J (1994) *Heart of Darkness.* London: Penguin Classics

De Angelis, R (1998) Globalization and recent higher education reform in Australia and France: Different constraints, differing choices in higher education structures, politics and policies, in: Hunt, I and Smyth, J (eds) *The Ethos of the University: West and beyond*, Bedford Park SA: Flinders University of South Australia

Dean, M (1994) *Critical and Effective Histories: Foucault's Methods and Historical Sociology.* London: Routledge

Dearing Report (1997) National Committee of Inquiry into Higher Education. Norwich: HMSO

Deleuze, G and Guattari, F (1988) *A Thousand Plateaus* (trans. Massumi, B) London: Athlone Press

DeMarco, R (1993) Mentorship: a feminist critique of current research, in: *Journal of Advanced Nursing* 18(8): 1242–1250

Denzin, N K (1997) *Interpretive Ethnography: Ethnographic Practices for the 21st Century.* Thousand Oaks CA: Sage

Denzin, N K and Lincoln, YS (1994) *Handbook of Qualitative Research.* Thousand Oaks CA: Sage

Department for Education and Employment (DfEE) (1998a) *Teaching: High Status, High Standards. Requirements for courses of initial teacher training (Circular 4/98)* London: DfEE

Department for Education and Employment (DfEE) (2000a) *Labour Market and Skill Trends 2000.* Nottingham: Skills and Enterprise Network/DfEE Publications, Ref: SEN 373

Department for Education and Employment (DfEE) (2001) *Skills for All: Proposals for a National Skills Agenda – Final Report of the National Skills Task Force.* Sudbury: DfEE Publications, Ref: SK728

Derrida, J (1976) *Of Grammatology* (trans: Spivak, G C) Baltimore: Johns Hopkins University Press (Original work published 1967)

Derrida, J (1978) *Writing and Difference.* (Trans: Bass, A). Chicago: University of Chicago Press (Originally published 1967)

Derrida, J (1978) *Writing and Difference.* London: Routledge

Derrida, J (1987) Letter to a Japanese friend, in: Kamuf, P (ed) (1991) *A Derrida Reader. Between the Blinds*. New York: Columbia University Press

Dewey, J (1939) *Freedom and Culture*. New York: Putman

Dillabough, J (2000) Women in teacher education: their struggles for inclusion as 'citizen-workers' in late modernity, in: Arnot, M and Dillabough, J (eds*)*, *Challenging Democracy: International Perspective on Gender, Education and Citizenship*. London: Routledge Falmer

Du Gay, P (1996) *Consumption and Identity at Work*. London: Sage

Ecclestone, K (1999) Care or control?: defining learners' needs for lifelong learning, in: *British Journal of Educational Studies* 47(4): 332–347

Edwards, R, Clarke, J, Harrison, R and Reeve, F (2001) Flexibility at work: a study of further education, in: *Journal of Vocational Education and Training*, 373–389

Edwards, R (1997) *Changing Places*. London: Routledge

Edwards, R (2001) Meeting Individual Learner Needs: power, subject, subjection, in: Paechter, C, Preedy, M, Scott, D and Soler, J (eds) *Knowledge, Power and Learning*. London: PCP

Eliot, T S (1958) *Four Quartets*. London: Faber

Eliot, T S (1973) *Selected Poems*. London: Faber

Elliot, J (2001) Making Evidence based Practice Educational, in: *British Educational Research Journal* 27(5): 555–574

Ellis, B (2001) The day the music dies. *HQ* August/September: 41

Ellis, C and Bochner, A P (2000) Autoethnography, Personal Narrative, Reflexivity, in: Denzin, N K and Lincoln, Y S (eds) *Handbook of Qualitative Research (2nd edn)*. London: Sage

Employment Support Unit (2000) *Mentoring Young People: Lessons from Youthstart*. Birmingham: Employment Support Unit

Eribon, D (1993) *Michel Foucault*. London: Faber

European Commission (EC) (1998) *Unlocking Young People's Potential*. Luxembourg: Office for Official Publications of the European Communities

Evans, K (2000) Beyond the work-related curriculum: citizenship and learning after sixteen, in: Bailey, R (ed) *Teaching Values and Citizenship Across the Curriculum*. London: Kogan Page

Evans, M (1997) Negotiating the Frontier: Women and Resistance in the Contemporary Academy? in: Stanley, L (ed), *Knowing Feminisms*. London: Sage

Fairclough, N (1992) *Discourse and Social Change*. London: Longman

Fang, Y (2001) Reporting the same events? A critical analysis of Chinese print news media texts, in: *Discourse and Society* 12(5): 585–613

Farnham, D (1999) Managing universities and regulating academic labour markets, in: Farnham, D (ed) *Managing Academic Staff in Changing University Systems: International trends and comparisons* Buckingham, PA: Open University Press

Farrell, H, James, B, Carmichael, E and Scoufis, M (1997) Critical practice and undergraduate students, in: Galobiowski, Z (ed) *Policy and Practice of Tertiary Literacy. Selected Proceedings of the First National Conference on Tertiary Literacy Volume 1*. Melbourne: Victoria University of Technology

Bibliography

Farrell, L (2000) Ways of doing, ways of being: Language, education and 'working' identities, in: *Language and Education* 14(1): 18–36

Featherstone, M (1996) Localism, globalism and cultural identity, in: Wilson, R and Dissanayake, W (eds) *Global Local: Cultural production and the transnational imaginary*. Durham: Duke University Press

Fielding, M (2001) Beyond the Rhetoric of Student Voice: new departures or new constraints in the transformation of 21st century schooling? in: *FORUM*, 43(2)

Forbes, A (2000) *Concepts of Mentoring*, lecture at the Manchester Metropolitan University, 1 February

Ford, G (1999) *Youthstart Mentoring Action Project: Project Evaluation and Report Part II*. Stourbridge: Institute of Careers Guidance

Foucault, M (1973) *The Order of Things: An archaeology of the human sciences*. New York: Vintage Books

Foucault, M (1977) *Discipline and Punish: The birth of the prison*. London: Penguin

Foucault, M (1978) *The Archaeology of Knowledge*. London: Tavistock

Foucault, M (1979) *The History of Sexuality Vol 1: Introduction*. Harmondsworth: Penguin

Foucault, M (1980) *Power/Knowledge; Selected Interviews and Other Writings 1972 – 1977*. Brighton: Harvester Press

Foucault, M (1986) *The Order of Things: An archaeology of the human sciences*. London: Tavistock

Foucault, M (1988) The political technology of individuals, in: Martin, L H, Gutman, H and Hutton, P H (eds) *Technologies of the Self: A Seminar with Michel Foucault*. Amherst: University of Massachusetts Press

Foucault, M (1991a) *Discipline and Punish: The birth of the prison*. London: Penguin

Foucault, M (1991b) Questions of Method, in: Burchell *at al* (eds) *The Foucault Effect: Studies in Governmentality*. Brighton: Harvester Wheatsheaf

Foucault, M (1998) Of Other Spaces, in: Mirzoeff, N *Visual Culture Reader*. London: Routledge

Foucault, M (2001) *Power: Essential Works of Foucault, 1954–1984, Vol. 3*. New York: The New Press

Freedman, M (1999) *The Kindness of Strangers: Adult Mentors, Urban Youth and the New Voluntarism*. Cambridge: Cambridge University Press

Freire, P (1970) *Pedagogy of the Oppressed*. London: Penguin

Freire, P (1996) *Letters to Christina*. London: Routledge

Friedman, T L (2000) *The Lexus and the Olive Tree: Understanding Globalization*. New York: Anchor Books

Frost, R (1971) Revelation, in: Lathem, E (ed) *The Poetry of Robert Frost*. London: Jonathan Cape

Gay, B and Stephenson, J (1998) The mentoring dilemma: guidance and/or direction? in: *Mentoring and Tutoring* 6(1): 43–54

Gerstner, L (2002) 'The Tests We Know We Need', in: *New York Times*, March 13: A 31

Giddens, A (1991) *Modernity and Self-Identity: Self and Society in the Late Modern Age.* Cambridge: Polity Press

Giddens, A (1998) *The Third Way: The Renewal of Social Democracy.* Cambridge: Polity Press

Giddens, A (1999) *Runaway World: How Globalisation is Reshaping our Lives.* London: Profile Books

Giroux, H (1992) *Border Crossings.* London: Routledge

Gleeson, D (1996) Post-compulsory education in a post-industrial and post-modern age, in: Avis, J, Bloomer, M Esland, G, Gleeson, D, and Hodkinson, P *Knowledge and Nationhood: Education, Politics and Work.* London: Cassell

Gleick, J (1988) *Chaos.* London: Heinemann

Glynn, C and Nairne, B (2000) *Young People's Attitudes to Work, Careers and Learning.* Horsham: Roffey Park

Golden, S and Sims, D (1997) *Review of Industrial Mentoring in Schools.* Slough: National Foundation for Educational Research

Goodnough, A (2000) 'Strain of Fourth-Grade Tests Drives Off Veteran Teachers', *New York Times,* June 14: A-1.

Goodson, I (1999) The Educational Researcher as a Public Intellectual, in: *British Educational Research Journal,* 25 (3): 277–299

Gordon, C (1991) Introduction, in: Graham, G, Gordon, C, and Miller, P *The Foucault Effect: studies in governmentality.* London: Harvester Wheatsheaf

Gordon, C (2001) Introduction, in Foucault, M *Power: Essential Works of Foucault, 1954–1984, Vol. 3.* New York: The New Press

Gore, J (1993) *The Struggle for Pedagogies: Critical and Feminist Discourses as Régimes of Truth.* New York: Routledge

Gramsci, A (1971) *Selections from the Prison Notebooks* (Edited and translated by Hoare, Q and Nowell Smith, G) New York: International Publishers

Green, B and Bigum, C (1990) Quantum Curriculum and Chaotic Classrooms: Re-Framing Educational Computing, in: McDougall, A and Dowling, C (eds) *Computers in Education.* North-Holland: Elsevier Science

Greenblatt, S (1998) Benefit of Clergy, Benefit of Literature, in: *Stanford Humanities Review* 6(1)

Gulam, W and Zulfiqar, M (1998) Mentoring – Dr. Plum's elixir and the alchemist's stone, in: *Mentoring and Tutoring* 5(3): 46–56

Habermas, J (1974) *Theory and Practice.* London: Heinemann

Habermas, J (1986) *The Theory of Communicative Action. Vol. 1. Reason and the Rationalization of Society.* Cambridge: Polity Press

Hacking, I (1986) Making up people, in: Heller, T C, Sosna, M and Wellbery, D (eds) *Reconstructing individualism: autonomy, individuality, and the self in Western thought.* Stanford: Stanford University Press

Hagar, P and Kaye, M (1992) Critical thinking in teacher education: A process-oriented research agenda, in: *Australian Journal of Teacher Education* 17(2): 22–23

Hamad, H (2002) Asians have the right to do things their way: Dr. M. *Business Times Malaysia* 4th December

Bibliography

Hall, S (1996) Who Needs 'Identity?' in: Hall, S and du Gay, P (eds) *Questions of Cultural Identity*. London: Sage

Hammersley, M (1997) Educational research and teaching: a response to David Hargreaves's TTA Lecture, in: *British Educational Research Journal* 23: 141–161

Haney, W (2000, August 19) 'The Myth of the Texas Miracle in Education', *Education Policy Analysis Archives*, available at epaa.asu.edu/epaa/v8n1.

Hardy, T (1972) *Jude the Obscure*. London: Macmillan

Hargreaves, D (1996) *Teaching as a research-based profession: possibilities and prospects*. Teacher Training Agency Annual Lecture. London: Teacher Training Agency

Harkin, J, Turner, G and Dawn, T (2001) *Teaching Young Adults. A handbook for teachers in post-compulsory education*. London: Routledge/Falmer

Harvey, D (2000) *Spaces of Hope*. Berkeley: University of California Press

Hayden, C (1999, Sept. 26th) Memo to W. Cala, superintendent of Fairport Central School District, Fairport, New York

Hayden, C (1999, Nov. 25) Reported in Gannet Press, cited in W. Cala letter to Deputy Commissioner of Education, New York, June 18, 2000

Hayden, C (2001, May 7) Letter to the Hon. Richard Brodsky and Hon. Richard Green, NY State Assembly

Hayes, D and Hudson, A (2001) *Basildon: The Mood of the Nation*. London: Demos

Hayes, D and Wynyard, R (2002a) Whimpering into the good night: Resisting McUniversity, in: Ritzer, G (ed) *The McDonaldization Reader*. Thousand Oaks CA: Sage

Hayes, D and Wynyard, R (2002b) Introduction, in Hayes, D and Wynyard, R (eds) *The McDonaldization of Higher Education*. Westport CT: Bergin and Garvey

Hayes, D (2002c) Taking the Hemlock: The Sophistry of Teacher Training for Higher Education, in: Hayes, D and Wynyard, R (eds) *The McDonaldization of Higher Education*. Westport CT: Bergin and Garvey

Hayes, D (2003) *The Rise of Therapeutic Education.* (forthcoming)

Heartfield, J (2002) *The 'Death of the Subject' Explained*. Sheffield: Sheffield Hallam University Press

Heidegger, M (1962) *Being and Time*. Oxford: Blackwell

Hertz, N (2001) *The Silent Takeover: Global Capitalism and the Death of Democracy*. London: Heinemann

Hey, V (1997) Northern Accent and Southern Comfort: Subjectivity and Social Class, in: Mahony, P and Zmroczek, C (eds) *Class Matters: 'Working-Class' Women's Perspectives on Social Class*. London: Taylor and Francis

Hey, V (2000) Troubling the Autobiography of the Questions, in: *Gender and Sexualities in Educational Ethnography*, 3: 161–183

Higgot, R and Nossal, K (1997) The international politics of liminality: relocating Australia in the Asia Pacific, in: *Australian Journal of Political Science* 32(2): 169–185

187

Hillocks, G Jr (2002) *The Testing Trap: How State Writing Assessments Control Learning.* New York: Teachers College Press

Hochschild, A R (1983) *The Managed Heart: Commercialization of Human Feeling.* Berkeley and Los Angeles: University of California Press

Hodge, M (2001) (interviewed by A. Goddard), Hodge puts her weight behind QAA, in: *Times Higher Educational Supplement,* 15 June: 1

Hodgson, A and Spours, K (eds) (1997) *New Labour's Educational Agenda. Issues and Policies for Education and Training from 14+.* London: Kogan Page

Hofstede, G (1980) *Culture's Consequences: International differences in work-related values.* Beverley Hills CA: Sage, in: Walker, A, Bridges, E and Chan, B (1996) Wisdom gained, wisdom given: Instituting PBL in a Chinese culture, in: *Journal of Educational Administration* 34(5): 12–31

Hollingdale, R J (ed) (1981) *A Nietzche Reader.* London: Penguin Classics

HEFCE (2001) Partnerships for Progression – Proposals by the HEFCE and the Learning and Skills Council. Consultation Document 01/73

hooks, b (1994) *Teaching to Transgress.* London: Routledge

hooks, b (2000) *Where we stand: class matters.* London: Routledge

House of Commons Education and Employment Committee (1998) *Disaffected Children Volume I: Report and Proceedings of the Committee.* London: The Stationery Office

Howarth, D (2000*) Discourse.* Buckingham: Open University Press

Huang, C (1997) *The Analacts of Confucius (Lun Yu). A literal Translation with an Introduction and Notes.* Oxford: Oxford University Press

Huddleston, P and Unwin, L (1997) *Teaching and Learning in Further Education.* London: Routledge

Hulbert, S (2000) *Working with Socially Excluded and 'At Risk' Young People: Research into the Need for, and Appropriate Form of, Support and Supervision for Personal Advisers Working Within the New Connexions Support Service.* Stourbridge: Institute of Career Guidance

Hursh, D (2001) Social Studies within the Neo-Liberal State: The Commodification of Knowledge and the End of Imagination, in: *Theory and Research in Social Education.* 29(2): 349–356

Industry in Education (1996) *Towards Employability: Addressing the Gap Between Young People's Qualities and Employers' Recruitment Needs.* London: Industry in Education

Irigaray, L (1974) *Speculum of the Other Woman.* Cornell: University Press

Irvine, Sir D (2001) Speech to the Royal Society of Medicine, *The Independent,* 16 January: 1

Jochnowitz, G (1986) Teaching at a provincial Chinese university *American Scholar* 55(4): 521–7, in: Pennycook, A (1998) *English and the Discourses of Colonialism.* New York: Routledge

Kamuf, P (ed) (1991) *A Derrida Reader. Between the Blinds.* New York: Columbia University Press

Kavanagh, J (2001) New Labour, New Millennium, New Premiership, in: Seldon, A (ed) (2001) *The Blair Effect.* London: Little Brown and Company

Bibliography

Keenan, D (1999) *Death and Responsibility: the 'work' of Levinas.* Albany: State University of New York Press

Kilpatrick, S, Bell, R and Falk, I (1999) The Role of Group Learning in Building Social Capital, in: *Journal of Vocational and Educational Training* 51(1): 129–144

Klein, N (2001) *No Logo.* London: Harper Collins

Kozol, J (2002) Malign Neglect, in: *The Nation* June 10th: 20. 22–23

Kram, K E (1988) *Mentoring at Work: Developmental Relationships in Organizational Life.* Lanham: University Press of America

Kuhn, T (1962) *The Structure of Scientific Revolutions.* Chicago: University of Chicago Press

Kumar, K (1995) *From Post-Industrial to Post-Modern Society: New Theories of the Contemporary World.* Oxford: Blackwell

Landry, D and MacLean, G (eds) (1996)*The Spivak Reader.* London: Routledge

Lane, J F (2000) *Pierre Bourdieu: A Critical Introduction.* London: Pluto Press

Lankshear, C (1994) *Critical Literacy.* Occasional paper no. 3. Belconnen, ACT: Australian Curriculum Studies Association

Lathem, E C (ed) (1971) *The Poetry of Robert Frost.* London: Jonathan Cape

Lather, P (1991) *Getting Smart: feminist research and pedagogy with/in the postmodern.* London: Routledge

Lather, P (1991) *Getting Smart: Feminist research and pedagogy with/in the postmodern.* New York: Routledge

Lather, P (2001) Working the Ruins of Feminist Ethnography *Signs* 27(1)

Lea, M and West, L (1995) Life Histories, Adult learning and Identity. in: Swindells, J (ed), *The Uses of Autobiography.* London: Taylor and Francis

Leonard, M (1994) Transforming the Household: Mature Women Students and Access to Higher Education. in: Davis, S, Lubelska, C and Quinn, J (eds), *Changing the Subject.* London: Taylor and Francis

Lescourret, M-A (1994) *Emmanuel Levinas.* Paris: Flammarion

Levinas, E (trans Cohen, R) (1985) *Ethics and Infinity: Conversations with Phillippe Nemo.* Pittsburgh: Duquesnes University Press

Levinas. E (1987) (trans Cohen, R) *Time and the Other.* Pittsburgh: Duquesne University Press

Levinas, E (1998) *Totality and Infinity: An Essay on Exteriority.* Pittsburgh: Duquesne University Press

Levinson, D J, Darrow, C N, Klein, E B, Levinson, M H and McKee, B (1978) *The Seasons of a Man's Life.* New York: Ballantine

Levitas, R (1996) The concept of social exclusion and the new Durkheimian hegemony, in: *Critical Social Policy* 16(1): 5–20

Liddicoat, A. (1997) Texts of the culture and texts of the discourse community, in: Golebiowski, Z and Borland, H (eds) *Academic Communication across Disciplines and Cultures. Selected Proceedings of the First National Conference on Tertiary Literacy Volume 2.* Melbourne: Victoria University of Technology

Lillis, T (2001) *Student Writing, Access, Regulation, Desire.* London: Routledge

Livingstone, K (2001) *A message from the Mayor,* Conference on Higher and

Further Education in London, London: 14th February

Long, J (1997) The dark side of mentoring, in: *Australian Educational Researcher* 24(2): 115–133

Losito, B, Pozzo, G and Somekh, B (1998) Exploring the Labyrinth of First and Second Order Inquiry in Action Research, in: *Educational Action Research* 6(2): 219–239

Lucas, N (2000) Towards professionalism: teaching in further education, in Gray, D E and Griffin, C (eds) *Post-Compulsory Education and the New Millennium*. London: Jessica Kingsley Publishers

Lukács, G (1968) *History and Class Consciousness*. London: Merlin Press

Lunneborg, P (1994) *OU Women*. London: Cassell

Luttrell, W (1997) *Schoolsmart and Motherwise*. London: Routledge

Lyotard, J-F (1984) *The Postmodern Condition: A Report on Knowledge*. Manchester: University Press

MacLure, M (1996) Exploring the transitions: boundary work in the lives of teacher-researchers, in: *British Educational Research Journal,* 22(3): 273–286

MacLure, M (1999) Discursive (il)literacy in research, policy and practice. Paper presented at the annual meeting of the British Educational Research Association, Brighton, September 1999

McCarthy, C and Dimitriades, G (2000) Governmentality and the sociology of education: media, education policy and the politics of resentment, in: *British Journal of Sociology of Education,* 21(2): 169–185

Maguire, M (1996) In the Prime of Their Lives? Older Women in Higher Education. in: Morley, L and Walsh, V (eds), *Breaking Boundaries: Women in Higher Education*. London: Taylor and Francis

Maguire, M (1997) Missing Links: Working-Class Women of Irish Descent, in: Mahony, P and Zmroczek, C (eds), *Class Matters: 'Working-Class' Women's Perspectives on Social Class*. London: Taylor and Francis

Maguire, M (1999) 'A Touch of Class': inclusion and exclusion in Initial Teacher Education, in: *Inclusive Education,* 3(1): 13–26

Maguire, M, Ball, S J and Macrae, S (2001) Post-adolescence, dependence and the refusal of adulthood, in: *Discourse* 22(2): 197–211

Majors, R, Wilkinson, V and Gulam, B (2000) Mentoring Black Males in Manchester, in: Owusu, K (ed) *Black British Culture and Society: A Text Reader*. London: Routledge

Margolis, J (1999) Pierre Bourdieu: *Habitus* and the Logic of Practice, in: Shusterman, R *Bourdieu: A Critical Reader*. Oxford: Blackwell

Marston, G (2000) Metaphor, morality and myth: a critical discourse analysis of public housing policy in Queensland, in: *Critical Social Policy* 20(3): 349–373

Marton, F, Hounsell, D and Entwhistle, N (eds) (1984) *The Experience of Learning*. Edinburgh: Scottish Academic Press

Marx, K and Engels, F (1872/1952 ed) *Manifesto of the Communist Party*. Moscow

Medhurst, A (2000) If Anywhere: Class Identifications and Cultural Studies Academics, in: Munt, S (ed), *Cultural Studies and the Working Class*. London: Cassell

Bibliography

Meek, J (2001) Why the management style of a Danish hearing-aid maker may hold the key to stopping Bin Laden, *The Guardian* 18 October, G2: 2–3

Megginson, D and Clutterbuck, D (1995) Mentoring in Action, in: Megginson, D and Clutterbuck, D (eds) *Mentoring in Action: A Practical Guide for Managers*. London: Kogan Page

Messer-Davidov, E (ed) (1993) *Knowledges: historical and critical studies in disciplinarity*. Virginia, USA: University of Virginia

Meyer, J H F and Kiley, M (1998) An exploration of Indonesian postgraduate students' conceptions of learning , in: *Journal of Further and Higher Education* 22(3): 287–298

Monk, D, Sipple, J and Killeen, K (2001, September 10) *Adoption and Adaptation, New York State School Districts' Responses to State Imposed High School Graduation Requirements: An Eight-Year Retroperspective*. Education Finance Research Consortium. Available at:
www.albany.edu/edfin/CR01_MSk_Report.pdf

Morgan, E and Burn, E (2000) Three perspectives on supporting a dyslexic trainee teacher, in: *Innovations in Education and Training International,* 37(2): 172–177

McNeil, L (2000) *Contradictions of School Reform: Educational Costs of Standardized Testing*. New York: Routledge Press

Miller, A (2002) *Mentoring For Students and Young People: A Handbook of Effective Practice*. London: Kogan Page

Milroy, J (1998) Children Can't Speak or Write Properly Anymore. In: Bauer, L and Trudgill, P (eds) *Language Myths*. London: Penguin

Minton, D (1991) *Teaching Skills in Further and Adult Education*. Basingstoke and London: Macmillan

Morley, L (1997) A Class of One's Own: Women, Social Class and the Academy, in: Mahony, P and Zmroczek, C (eds*), Class Matters: Working-Class Women's Perspectives on Social Class*. London: Taylor and Francis

Morris, E (2001) Professionalism and Trust: the future of teachers and teaching. A speech by the Rt Hon Estelle Morris MP, Secretary of State for Education and Skills, to the Social Market Foundation, 12th November, 2001. London: Department for Education and Skills

Nardelli, M (2001) Plugging Australia's brain drain, in: *Unisa News* May
http: //www.unisa.edu.au/mdu/unisanews_may2001/plugging.htm

New York Performance Standards Consortium (2001) Petition to the New York State Supreme Court. Retrieved June 2, 2002 from the Coalition for Common Sense website: http: //freespeech.org/ccse

New York State Education Department (2002) History of the University of the State of New York and the State Education Department 1984–1996: James Folts. Retrieved 30.11.02 from
http//www.nysl.nysed.gov: 80/edocs/education/sedhist/htm

Newby, H (2002) Address to HEFCE Annual Conference Manchester Institute of Science and Technology, April 18

Nicholson, W (2000) *The Wind Singer*. London: Mammoth

Nolan, J L (1998) *The Therapeutic State: Justifying Government at Century's*

End. New York: New York University Press

Norris, C (1991) *Deconstruction: Theory and Practice* (revised edition). London: Routledge

Oakley, A (2001) Making Evidence-based Practice Educational: a rejoinder to John Elliot, in: *British Educational Research Journal*, 27(5): 575–576

Paechter, C *et al* (2001) *Knowledge, Power and Learning*. London: Sage

Palshaugen, O (2001) The Use of Words: Improving enterprises by improving their conversations, in: Reason, P and Bradbury, H (eds) *Handbook of Action Research*. London: Sage

Parenti, C (1999) Atlas Finally Shrugged: Us Against Them in the Me Decade, in: *The Baffler*, 13, 108–120

Parker, D and Stacey, R (1984) *Chaos, Management and Economics: The Implications of Non-Linear Thinking*. London: Institute of Economic Affairs

Parker, J (1999) School policies and practices: the teacher's role, in: Cole, M (ed) *Professional Issues for Teachers and Student Teachers*. London: David Fulton Publishers

Pennycook, A (1998) *English and the Discourses of Colonialism*. New York: Routledge

Peters, M (1994) Individualism and Community: Education and the Politics of Difference, in: *Discourse*, 14(2)

Peters, T and Waterman, R (1982) *In Search of Excellence: Lessons from America's Best-Run Companies*. New York: Warne Books

Philip, K and Hendry, L B (1996) Young people and mentoring – towards a typology? in: *Journal of Adolescence* 19(3): 189–201

Pilger, J (2002) *The New Rulers of the World*. London: Verso

Piper, H and Piper, J (2000) Disaffected Young People as the problem. Mentoring as the solution. Education and work as the goal, in: *Journal of Education and Work* 13(1): 77–94

Plant, S (1998) *Zeroes and Ones*. London: Fourth Estate

Plato (1955) *The Republic*. Oxford: Oxford University Press

Plato (1989) *Phaedrus and Letters VII and VIII*. London: Penguin Classics

Plummer, G (2000) *Failing Working-Class Girls*. Stoke on Trent: Trentham Books

Plumwood, V (1993) Dualism: the logic of colonisation. In *Feminism and the Mastery of Nature*. London: Routledge

Popkewitz, T S (2000) The denial of change in educational change: systems of ideas in the construction of national policy and evaluation, in: *Educational Researcher*, 29(1): 19–29

Prigogine, I and Stengers, I (1985) *Order Out of Chaos*. London: Fontana

Proust, M (1983) *Remembrance of Things Past*. London: Penguin

Puiggros, A (1999) *Neoliberalism and Education in Latin America*. Boulder, CO: Westview Press

Purdie, N, Hattie, J and Douglas, G (1996) Student conceptions of learning and their use of self-regulated learning strategies: a cross-cultural comparison, in: *Journal of Educational Psychology* 88(1): 87–100

Quinn, J (2001) Curriculum: the Hidden Issue in the Access to Higher Education

Bibliography

Debate, paper presented at BERA conference, Leeds University, September 13–15

Quinn, J (2003) *Powerful Subjects*: *Are Women Really Taking Over the University?* Stoke on Trent: Trentham Books

Quinn, J (forthcoming) *Inside the Box*: *The role of research within widening participation partnerships*

Rabinow, P (ed) (1984) *The Foucault Reader. An introduction to Foucault's thought.* London: Penguin

Ransom, J (1997) *Foucault's Discipline*: *The Politics of Subjectivity.* Duke University Press

Readings, B (1996) *The University in Ruins.* Cambridge Mass: Harvard University Press

Reay, D (1997) The Double-Bind of the 'Working-Class' Feminist Academic: The Success of Failure or the Failure of Success? In: Mahony, P and Zmroczek, C (eds), *Class Matters*: *'Working-Class' Women's Perspectives on Social Class.* London: Taylor and Francis

Reay, D. (1998) *Class Work.* London: UCL Press

Reed, E (1975) *Woman's Evolution.* New York: Pathfinder Press

Rikowski, G (2001) Education for industry: a complex technicism, in: *Journal of Education and Work* 14(1): 29–49

Reeves, F (ed) (1997) *Further Education as Economic Regeneration*: *The Starting Point.* Bilston: Bilston Community College and Education and Now Books

Roberts, A (1999) An historical account to consider the origins and associations of the term mentor, in: *History of Education Society Bulletin* (64) 313–329

Roberts, A (2000a) Mentoring revisited: a phenomenological reading of the literature, in: *Mentoring and Tutoring* 8(2): 145–170

Roberts, A (2000b) *The Androgynous Mentor*: *An Examination of Mentoring Behaviour Within an Educational Context.* Unpublished PhD thesis, University of Birmingham

Robertson, S (2000) *A Class Act*: *Changing teachers' work, the State, and globalization* New York: Falmer Press

Robson, J (2000) A Profession in Crisis: Status, Culture and Identity in the Further Education College, in: Hall, L and Marsh, K (eds) *Professionalism, Policies and Values.* London: Greenwich University Press

Rose, N (1996) *Inventing Ourselves*: *Psychology, Power, Personhood.* Cambridge: Cambridge University Press

Rose, N (1999) *Powers of Freedom*: *Reframing Political Thought.* Cambridge: Cambridge University Press

Ross, E W (1999) Resisting the Test Mania, in: *Z Magazine* 12(9): 21–22

Rowland, S (1984) *The Enquiring Classroom.* Lewis: Falmer

Rowland, S (2000) *The Enquiring University Teacher.* Milton Keynes: Society for Research into Higher Education and Open University Press

Rowland, S (2002) Overcoming fragmentation in professional life: the challenge for academic development, *Higher Education Quarterly*, 56(1): 52–64

St. Pierre, E A (1997a) Methodology in the fold and the irruption of transgressive data, in: *International Journal of Qualitative Studies in Education,* 10(2): 175–189

St. Pierre, E A (1997b). An introduction to figurations – a poststructural practice of inquiry, *International Journal of Qualitative Studies in Education,* 10(3): 279–284

St. Pierre, E A (2001a) The intelligibility of postmodern educational research. Paper presented at the annual meeting of the American Educational Research Association, Seattle, 10th–14th April

St. Pierre, E A (2001b) Ethics under deconstruction. Paper presented at the annual meeting of the American Educational Research Association, Seattle, 10th–14th April

Saussure, F de (1966) *Course in General Linguistics.* London: McGraw-Hill

Scandura, T A (1998) Dysfunctional mentoring relationships and outcomes, *Journal of Management* 24(3): 449–467

Schön, D (1983) *The Reflective Practitioner.* San Francisco: Jossey Bass

Schön, D (1983) *The Reflective Practitioner: How Professionals Think in Action.* New York: Basic Books

Schuller, T (1995) *The Changing University?* Milton Keynes: Society for Research into Higher Education and Open University Press

Seldon, A (2001) The Net Blair Effect, in: Seldon, A (ed) (2001) *The Blair Effect.* London: Little Brown and Company

Skeggs, B (1994) Situating the production of feminist ethnography , in: Maynard, M and Purvis, J (eds) *Researching Women's Lives from a Feminist Perspective.* London: Taylor and Francis

Skeggs, B (1997a) Classifying Practices: Representations, Capitals and Recognitions, in: Mahony, P and Zmroczek, C (eds), *Class Matters: 'Working-Class' Women's Perspectives on Social Class.* London: Taylor and Francis

Skeggs, B (1997b.) *Formations of Class and Gender.* London: Sage

Skinner, A and Fleming, J (1999) *Mentoring socially excluded young people: Lessons from practice.* Manchester: National Mentoring Network

Smith, M and Scoll, B (1995) The Clinton Human Capital Agenda, in: *Teachers College Record* 96 Spring: 389–404

Smith, N (ed) *Standards Mean Business.* National Alliance of Business

Smithers, A (2001) 'Education Policy', in: Seldon, A (ed) (2001) *The Blair Effect.* London: Little Brown and Company

Social Exclusion Unit (1999) *Bridging the Gap: New Opportunities for 16–18 Year Olds.* London: The Stationery Office

Spizzica, M (1997) Cultural differences within 'Western' and 'Eastern' education, in: Golebiowski, Z and Borland, H (eds) *Academic Communication across Disciplines and Cultures. Selected Proceedings of the First National Conference on Tertiary Literacy Vol 2* Melbourne: Victoria University of Technology

Spours, K and Lucas, N (1996) *The Formation of a National Sector of Incorporated Colleges: Beyond the FEFC Model. Working Paper No 19,* London: Institute of Education, University of London

Squires, G (1987) The Curriculum, in: Becher, T (ed) *British Higher Education.*

Bibliography

London: Allen and Unwin

Stacey, J (1988) Can there be a Feminist Ethnography? in: *Women's Studies International Forum* 11(1): 21–27

Stake, R E (1995) *The Art of Case Study Research.* London: Sage

Stammers, P (1992) The Greeks had a word for it . . . (five millennia of mentoring), in: *British Journal of In-Service Education* 18(2): 76–80

Standing, M (1999) Developing a Supportive/Challenging and Reflective/Competency Education (SCARCE) mentoring model and discussing its relevance to nurse education, in: *Mentoring and Tutoring* 6(3): 3–17

Stenhouse, L (1975) *An Introduction to Curriculum Research and development.* London: Heinemann

Strathern, M (2000) The tyranny of transparency, *British Educational Research Journal,* 26(3): 309–321

Stronach, I (1989) A critique of the 'new assessment': from currency to carnival? in: Simons, H and Elliott, J (eds) *Rethinking Appraisal and Assessment.* Buckingham: Open University Press

Stronach, I (1996) Fashioning post-modernism, finishing modernism: tales from the fitting room, in: *British Educational Research Journal,* 22(3): 359–375

Stronach, I (1999) On being the nation again. SERA lecture. Annual meeting of the Scottish Educational Research Association, Dundee, October 1999

Stronach, I and MacLure, M (1997) *Educational Research Undone: The postmodern embrace.* Buckingham: Open University Press

Tester, K (1994) *The Flâneur.* London: Routledge

Tett, L (2000) 'I'm Working Class and Proud of It' – gendered experiences of non-traditional participants in higher education., in: *Gender and Education.* 1(2): 183–194

Therborn, G (1978) The Frankfurt School, in: New Left Review (eds) *Western Marxism: A Critical Reader.* London: Verso

Thomas, E, Quinn, J, Slack, K and Williams, S (2001) *Evaluation of partnerships to widen participation.* Bristol: HEFCE

Thomas, E, Cooper, M and Quinn, J (2002) *Collaboration to widen participation.* Stoke on Trent: Trentham Books

Thompson, J (2000) *Women, Class and Education.* London: Routledge

Thompson, S (1998) Who Goes There, Friend or Foe? Black Women, White Women and Friendships in Academia, in: Malinda, D and Maslin-Protheroe, S (eds), *Surviving the Academy.* London: Falmer Press

Tomlinson, S (2000) Labour's Narrow Vision: A Comment on Michael Barber's speech at the Smith Richardson Foundation, Washington, in: *Education and Social Justice* 3(1) Autumn, 2–5

Traub. J (2002) 'The Test Mess', *New York Times Magazine,* April 7: 46–51, 60, 78

Tripp, D (1993) *Critical Incidents in Teaching.* London: Routledge

Usher, R and Edwards, R (1994) *Postmodernism and Education.* London: Routledge

Usher, R and Edwards, R (1998) Confessing all? A 'postmodern' guide to the guidance and counselling of adult learners, in: Edwards, R, Harrison, R, and

Tait, A (eds) *Telling Tales: Perspectives on Guidance and Counselling in Learning*. London: Routledge

Van Maanen, J (1988*) Tales of the Field: On Writing Ethnography*. Chicago: University of Chicago Press

Venturino, S (2000) Globalization, cultural critique and China, in: *Social Semiotics* 10(2): 211–220

Vilas, C (1996) Neoliberal Social Policy: Managing Poverty (Somehow), in: *NACLA Report on the Americas*, 29(2): 16–21

Walker, A, Bridges, E and Chan, B (1996) Wisdom gained, wisdom given: Instituting PBL in a Chinese culture, in: *Journal of Educational Administration* 34(5): 12–31

Walker, S (1999) Bridging my Dangerous Gap: a personal maths story, in: *Primary Teaching Studies* Volume 10. Number 2.

Walkerdine, V (1992) Progressive pedagogy and political struggle, in: Luke, C and Gore, J (eds) *Feminisms and Critical Pedagogy*. London: Routledge

Walkerdine, V, Lucey, H and Melody, J (2001) *Growing Up Girl*. Basingstoke: Palgrave

Walklin, L (1990) *Teaching and Learning in Further and Adult Education*. Cheltenham: Stanley Thornes

Walsh, V (1996) Terms of Engagement: Pedagogy as a Healing Politic, in: Morley, L and Walsh, V (eds) *Breaking Boundaries: Women in Higher Education*. London: Taylor and Francis

Watt, S and Paterson, L C (2000) Pathways and Partnerships: widening access to higher education, in: *Journal of Further and Higher Education*, 24(1): 107–116

Weber, C (2002) Pavis Lecture, Open University

West, L (1999) *Beyond Fragments*. London: Taylor Francis

Whitehead, A N (1929) *The Aims of Education*. New York: Mentor Books

Wickert, R (1997) What does it mean, to 'have a policy'? The case of adult literacy in Australia, in: *Australian Educational Researcher* 24(2): 23–41

Winter, R (1996) New Liberty, New Discipline, in: Cuthbert, R (ed) *Working in Higher Education*. Milton Keynes: Society for Research into Higher Education and Open University Press

Wise, S (1997) What are Feminist Academics For? in: Stanley, L (ed) *Knowing Feminisms*. London: Sage

Wittgenstein, L (1922) *Tractatus Logico-Philosophicus*. London: Routledge

Wittgenstein, L (1978) *The Philosophical Investigations*. London: Blackwell

Woods, M (2001) Just one of those ends, in: *London Review of Books* 13 December: 9–11

Yarrow, K and Esland, G (1999) *The Changing Role of the Professional in the New Further Education*. Milton Keynes, Open University: CSSR Paper

Index